GCSE AQA
Physical Education

This brilliant CGP book has everything you need to get a top GCSE PE grade!

We've included clear explanations and exam-style questions on the whole AQA course, plus a couple of handy online extras. Yep — this book also comes with access to fun quizzes and knowledge organisers that summarise every topic!

We've even added a free Online Edition to read on your PC, Mac or tablet.

Unlock your Digital Extras

Just scan a QR code in the book to get your digital extras. Or go to **cgpbooks.co.uk/extras** and enter this code to unlock your Online Edition!

4047 1544 5571 7604

By the way, this code only works for one person. If somebody else has used this book before you, they might have already claimed the code.

Complete
Revision & Practice

Includes Free Online Edition, Digital Quizzes & Knowledge Organisers!

Contents

Throughout this book you'll see grade stamps like these:

These grade stamps help to show how difficult the questions are.
Remember — to get a top grade you need to be able to answer **all** the questions, not just the hardest ones.

On the question pages of this book, extended writing questions are marked like this: 1

Contents

This book includes digital extras — just scan the QR code to access them! You'll find a **Knowledge Organiser** and an **Online Quiz** for every topic.

P.S. You can also find these extras at: **cgpbooks.co.uk/Ocean**

Digital Extras

Published by CGP

From original material by Paddy Gannon.

Editors:
Liam Dyer, Mary Falkner, Josie Gilbert, Nathan Leach, Alison Palin, Claire Plowman and Maddie Wright.

With thanks to Camilla Sheridan for the proofreading.

With thanks to Jade Sim for the copyright research.

Acknowledgements:

Definition of health on page 33 is reproduced from the WHO website, The Constitution of the World Health Organization https://www.who.int/about/governance/constitution. Accessed: 2nd October 2023.

Normative data table for grip dynamometer test on pages 40 & 42 is used with permission of Elsevier Science & Technology Journals, from Physical education and the study of sport, Bob Davis, 4th edition, 2000, permission conveyed through Copyright Clearance Center, Inc.

Graphs on pages 73, 105 & 128 © Sport England 2023.

Source for the data about shirt sponsorship in the Premier League on pages 76 & 104: Sporting Intelligence 'sportingintelligence.com'.

ISBN: 978 1 78908 008 7
Printed by Bell & Bain Ltd, Glasgow.
Clipart from Corel®

Answering Exam Questions

Before you get on with your PE revision, here are some handy tips about **what to expect** in your **exams**. There's also some advice on how to get **top marks** in all the **different types** of PE exam question, which you can put into practice as you work through this book.

You'll Sit **Two Exams** for PE

Each paper will be worth <u>78 marks</u> and will last <u>1 hour 15 minutes</u>:

In total, your exams will make up 60% of your GCSE PE mark.

PAPER 1

1) <u>Paper 1</u> will test you on 'The human body and movement in physical activity and sport.'

2) It includes the topics:
   - Applied anatomy and physiology
   - Movement analysis
   - Physical training
   - Use of data

3) The first three topics are covered in <u>sections 1–3</u> of this book (pages 4-58). 'Use of data' is in <u>section 7</u> (pages 100-106).

PAPER 2

1) <u>Paper 2</u> will test you on 'Socio-cultural influences and well-being in physical activity and sport.'

2) It includes the topics:
   - Sports psychology
   - Socio-cultural influences
   - Health, fitness and well-being
   - Use of data

3) The first three topics are covered in <u>sections 4–6</u> of this book (pages 59-99). 'Use of data' is in <u>section 7</u> (pages 100-106).

There are **Three** Types of Question you could be asked

Multiple-Choice Questions — **Shade** the Right Oval

1) The multiple-choice questions give you a choice of <u>four</u> possible answers to the question. All you need to do is <u>shade</u> in the oval next to the <u>correct answer</u>. They're worth <u>one mark</u> each.

2) Make sure you only shade <u>one</u> oval — if you shade more than one you won't get the mark.

3) Don't worry if you make a <u>mistake</u> and want to change your answer. Just <u>cross</u> out the <u>wrong answer</u>, then <u>shade</u> in the oval next to your new answer.

There will be instructions on how to change your answer in the exam too.

4) If you <u>don't know</u> the answer to a question, <u>guess</u>. You don't lose marks for putting a wrong answer — if you guess, you've at least got a <u>chance</u> of getting it right.

Short-Answer Questions

1) <u>Short-answer</u> questions are usually worth between <u>one</u> and <u>four</u> marks.

2) Make sure you <u>read the question</u> carefully. For example, if you're asked for two influences, make sure you give <u>two</u>, otherwise you won't get all the marks.

3) To get the marks, you'll need to <u>show</u> your <u>PE knowledge</u>, <u>apply</u> it to a situation, or use it to <u>analyse</u> or <u>evaluate</u> something. In questions worth more marks, you might need to do a <u>combination</u> of these.

Extended Writing Questions

1) <u>Extended writing</u> questions are worth a whopping <u>six</u> or <u>nine</u> marks.

2) To answer these questions, as well as <u>showing</u> and <u>applying</u> your PE knowledge, you'll need to weigh up the <u>advantages</u> and <u>disadvantages</u> of something, or <u>analyse</u> how or why something happens.

3) At the end of your answer, you might need to write a <u>conclusion</u> where you make a <u>judgement</u>.

You'll also be assessed on '<u>how well you write your answer</u>', so make sure you do these things:

- <u>Organise</u> your answer — jot down what you want to cover in a quick <u>plan</u> before you start writing it. That way you can <u>structure</u> your answer well, and cover all the points you need to in a <u>logical</u> way.

- <u>Answer the question</u> being asked — stay focused on the topic you're asked about, and don't waffle about anything that's <u>not relevant</u>.

- Write in <u>full sentences</u> and use the correct <u>spelling</u>, <u>grammar</u> and <u>punctuation</u>.

- Use the correct <u>PE vocabulary</u>.

Answering Exam Questions

You get **Marks** for Meeting Different **Assessment Objectives**

1) <u>Assessment objectives</u> (<u>AOs</u>) are the things you need to do to <u>get marks</u> in the exams.
2) You'll be tested on <u>three</u> AOs:

> <u>**Assessment objective 1**</u> (AO1) is all about <u>demonstrating knowledge</u> and <u>understanding</u> of a topic.
> 1) Questions that test AO1 usually ask you to <u>state</u>, <u>define</u>, <u>describe</u>, <u>outline</u> or <u>identify</u> something.
> 2) They could also get you to <u>complete</u> a table or <u>draw</u> / <u>label</u> a diagram or graph.

> <u>**Assessment objective 2**</u> (AO2) is about <u>applying knowledge</u> and <u>understanding</u> of a topic to a context.
> 1) Questions that assess AO2 might ask you to <u>explain why</u> or <u>how</u> something happens.
> 2) You'll sometimes need to <u>give examples</u> or <u>suggest reasons</u> to back up your points.

> <u>**Assessment objective 3**</u> (AO3) is about <u>analysing</u> and <u>evaluating</u>.
> 1) Questions that test AO3 often start with words like <u>analyse</u>, <u>evaluate</u>, <u>discuss</u> or <u>justify</u>.
> 2) <u>Analysing</u> just means breaking something down into <u>parts</u> or <u>stages</u> to explain it. This can include <u>analysing data</u> to explain what it <u>shows</u>.
> 3) To <u>evaluate</u> or <u>discuss</u> something, you will need to weigh up its <u>advantages</u> and <u>disadvantages</u> in the context given in the question.
> 4) <u>Justifying</u> something means giving reasons <u>why</u> it's sensible.

3) A lot of questions, especially <u>extended writing questions</u>, will test <u>more than one</u> assessment objective — for example, if a question tells you to <u>evaluate</u> something (AO3), you'll also need to <u>demonstrate</u> your knowledge of the topic (AO1) and <u>apply it</u> to the situation in the question (AO2).

This <u>example exam answer</u> will show you how <u>marks</u> are awarded for the things you write:

> 15 **Figure 1** shows a performer taking part in archery.
> Evaluate the importance of agility to the archer.
>
>
> **Figure 1**
>
> AO1 → *Agility is the ability to change body position or direction quickly and with control.*
> AO2 → *Archers need to keep their body in a still, steady position so that they can aim accurately at the target.*
> *Therefore, agility is not an important component of fitness for an archer.* ← AO3
>
> **[3 marks]**

- This answer gets <u>one mark</u> for each <u>assessment objective</u> it meets.
- It meets AO1 by <u>defining agility</u>, AO2 by explaining what <u>impact</u> agility has on an archer, and AO3 by <u>evaluating</u> the importance of agility for the archer.

Answering Exam Questions

Read the Questions and Don't Panic

1) Read every question carefully.

2) The number of marks each question is worth is shown next to it in brackets. This can be a good guide to the number of points you need to make and how long your answer should be.

3) Make sure your answers are clear and easy to read. If the examiner can't read your handwriting, they won't be able to give you any marks.

4) Don't panic — if you get stuck on a question, just move on to the next one. You can come back to it if you have time at the end.

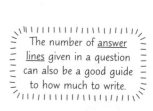
The number of answer lines given in a question can also be a good guide to how much to write.

Have a look at this Example Question and Answer

This example exam answer will show you how you might answer one of the extended writing questions.

15 Outline what continuous training and plyometric training are and evaluate whether they can improve performance in cycling.

This applies knowledge of continuous training to the cyclist by saying what impact it will have on their performance.

This looks at the disadvantages of continuous training by talking about aspects of cycling performance that it doesn't improve.

These points evaluate the effects of plyometric training on performance.

_____ Continuous training involves exercising aerobically for at least twenty minutes, and helps to improve both muscular endurance and cardiovascular endurance. Good muscular endurance would help to prevent muscle fatigue when cycling long distances, and a high level of cardiovascular endurance would allow a cyclist to cycle continuously for long periods. Continuous training is very important for preparing a cyclist for long races. It can also be included as part of a normal cycling training session, allowing a cyclist to practise their overall technique. However, continuous training involves exercising at a steady rate, so would not prepare a cyclist for the differing intensities involved in the sport, for example, when cycling on steep gradients, or during a sprint finish in a race.

_____ Plyometric training involves exercises such as jumping, to improve power in the legs. Power is an important component of fitness in cycling, as it is used to pedal forcefully and quickly, helping a cyclist to maintain a high speed. Power is very important during a race as it allows a cyclist to accelerate quickly, so they can overtake other riders. However, plyometric training alone is not the most suitable training method for a cyclist, as it does not provide practice of sport-specific actions, such as pedalling technique.

_____ A combination of continuous and plyometric training would be very useful for a cyclist wishing to improve their performance. However, a cyclist wishing to improve their performance further might also use interval training, which would improve their ability to exercise at high intensities.

This shows good knowledge of continuous training by talking about the components of fitness that it improves.

These points evaluate the effects of continuous training on performance.

This shows knowledge of plyometric training and applies it to the cyclist's performance.

In your evaluation, you can also mention other training methods needed for cycling.

[9 marks]

The Skeletal System

Welcome to the GCSE PE fun bus — first stop is the **skeleton**. It gives the body its **shape** and has loads of **jobs** to do. It's made up of various kinds of **bones**, all with their own function. Here we go...

The **Skeleton** has Different **Functions**

The skeleton does <u>more</u> than you might think to help your performance in sport. Its main functions are:

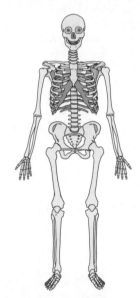

① **SUPPORT/SHAPE**:
- The skeleton is a <u>rigid bone frame</u> for the rest of the body. Our <u>shape</u> is mainly due to our <u>skeleton</u>.
- The skeleton <u>supports</u> the <u>soft tissues</u> like skin and muscle.
- This helps you to have good <u>posture</u>, which is <u>essential</u> in loads of sports.
- E.g. good posture aids <u>performance</u> in <u>gymnastics</u>.

② **PROTECTION**:
- Bones are very <u>tough</u> — they <u>protect vital organs</u> like the <u>brain</u>, <u>heart</u> and <u>lungs</u>.
- This allows you to <u>perform well</u> in sport without fear of serious <u>injury</u>.
- E.g. the <u>skull</u> protects the brain, so you can <u>head</u> a football or take punches in a boxing match <u>without serious injury</u>.

③ **MOVEMENT**:
- <u>Muscles</u>, <u>attached</u> to bones by <u>tendons</u>, can <u>move</u> bones at <u>joints</u>.
- This movement is essential for good <u>performance</u> in sport.
- There are different <u>types of movement</u> at the various <u>joints</u>, which are important in <u>different sports</u>.

④ **MAKING BLOOD CELLS**:
- Some <u>bones</u> contain <u>bone marrow</u>, which makes the components of <u>blood</u> — red and white <u>blood cells</u> (see p.13).
- <u>Red blood cells</u> are really <u>important</u> during exercise — they transport the <u>oxygen</u> that muscles need to move.
- Athletes with <u>more</u> red blood cells <u>perform better</u> — <u>more oxygen</u> can be delivered to their muscles.

⑤ **MINERAL STORAGE**:
- Bones store <u>minerals</u> like <u>calcium</u> and <u>phosphorus</u>.
- These help with <u>bone strength</u> — so you're less likely to <u>break</u> a bone.
- They're also needed for <u>muscle contraction</u> — so the body can <u>move</u>.

There are Different **Types** of Bone in the Skeleton

There are <u>three</u> main types of bone in the skeleton. Each type is <u>suited</u> to a different <u>purpose</u>.

LONG BONES

<u>Long</u> bones (e.g. the humerus in the arm) are used for larger <u>gross movements</u>.

SHORT BONES

<u>Short</u> bones are used for smaller <u>fine movements</u> — e.g. bones in the hand moving at the wrist.

FLAT BONES

Flat bones (e.g. the ribs) <u>protect</u> internal organs. Their broad surface also allows <u>muscle attachment</u>.

<u>Short</u> bones are also <u>weight-bearing</u> — e.g. the talus in the foot supports the weight of the body. <u>Long</u> bones can be used as <u>lever arms</u> (see p.27) and are strong, e.g. moving the leg at the hip.

The skeleton does more than you think in PE...

Those five functions of the skeleton are crucial in helping you perform in physical activity and sport. Try writing down an example of how each function could help performance in one sport.

The Skeletal System

Time for some more skeleton-related fun — this page'll give you a hand at remembering the **names** of some **important bones** in the body, their types and **what they do**. I bet you can hardly wait...

Learn the Structure of the Skeleton

Luckily, you don't need to know all 206 bones in the human body — just some of the <u>main ones</u>. But you might be asked to give an example of a <u>sporting movement</u> that uses a particular <u>type of bone</u>.

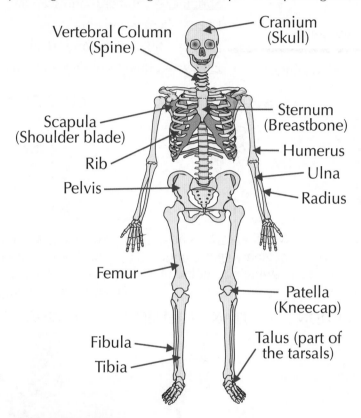

Vertebral Column (Spine)
Cranium (Skull)
Scapula (Shoulder blade)
Sternum (Breastbone)
Rib
Humerus
Pelvis
Ulna
Radius
Femur
Patella (Kneecap)
Fibula
Talus (part of the tarsals)
Tibia

LONG BONES

<u>Humerus</u> — used by muscles to <u>move</u> the <u>whole</u> arm, e.g. swinging a badminton racket.

<u>Ulna</u> and <u>radius</u> — used by muscles to <u>move</u> the <u>lower</u> arm, e.g. bending at the elbow to throw a netball.

<u>Femur</u> — used by muscles to <u>move</u> the <u>whole</u> leg, e.g. when walking or running.

<u>Fibula</u> and <u>tibia</u> — used by muscles to <u>move</u> the <u>lower</u> leg, e.g. to kick a football.

FLAT BONES

<u>Cranium</u> — <u>protects</u> the brain.

<u>Sternum</u> and <u>ribs</u> — <u>protect</u> the heart and lungs. The ribs also protect the kidneys.

<u>Scapula</u> — <u>protects</u> the shoulder joint and has many <u>muscles</u> attached to it, helping arm and shoulder <u>movement</u>.

<u>Pelvis</u> — <u>protects</u> the reproductive organs and the bladder. It also has many muscles attached to it, helping leg <u>movement</u>.

SHORT BONES

<u>Talus</u> — bears the body's <u>weight</u> when on foot, e.g. during standing and running. It is part of a group of bones called the <u>tarsals</u>.

OTHER BONES

The <u>vertebral column</u> (spine) is made up of <u>irregular</u> bones called <u>vertebrae</u> that protect the <u>spinal cord</u>.

The <u>patella</u> is a <u>sesamoid bone</u>. It protects the <u>tendon</u> that crosses the knee joint by stopping it <u>rubbing</u> against the femur.

Cranium, scapulas, patellas and toes, patellas and toes...

... Not quite as catchy. It's important that you learn all the bones shown on the diagram — you might have to identify the bones at a joint, link bones to their function, or suggest sporting actions that use them.

The Skeletal System

Joints are really important parts of the skeleton — you need to know **what they are**, how they can **move** and what **types** of joints you'll find in the body. Luckily, all that is right here on this page.

There are **Different Kinds** of Joint Movement

1) Joints are any points where two or more bones meet. The bones that meet at a joint are called the articulating bones of the joint.

2) Here are a few examples of some of the major joints in the body, and their articulating bones: ➡️

Hip — pelvis and femur
Shoulder — humerus and scapula
Knee — femur and tibia
Ankle — tibia, fibula and talus
Elbow — humerus, radius and ulna

3) There are eight joint movements that you need to know:

FLEXION

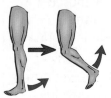

Closing a joint, e.g. the elbow in preparation for a basketball throw.

EXTENSION

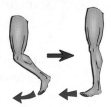

Opening a joint, e.g. kicking a football.

ADDUCTION

Moving towards an imaginary centre line, e.g. swinging a golf club.

ABDUCTION

Moving away from an imaginary centre line, e.g. taking back a tennis racket before swinging it.

ROTATION

Clockwise or anticlockwise movement of a limb, e.g. the shoulder movement during a top spin forehand in tennis.

CIRCUMDUCTION

Movement of a limb, hand or foot in a circular motion, e.g. bowling a cricket ball overarm.

PLANTAR FLEXION

Extension at the ankle, e.g. pointing the toes during gymnastics.

DORSIFLEXION

Flexion at the ankle, e.g. lifting the toes during gymnastics.

There are Different **Joint Types** in the Body

You need to know about two types of joint — ball and socket and hinge.
Each type allows a certain range of movements.

type	examples	flexion and extension	adduction and abduction	rotation	circumduction
ball and socket	hip, shoulder	✓	✓	✓	✓
hinge	knee, ankle, elbow	✓	✗	✗	✗

Plantar flexion and dorsiflexion are the names for extension and flexion at the ankle.

Each joint type has a different range of movement...

Make sure you don't get adduction and abduction mixed up — ADDuction brings two bits together, like adding them. ABDuction takes them away — like being abducted by aliens.

The Skeletal System

Coming up on this page — a little more on **joint movements**, and the different things joints are **made** of. As well as bones, joints have other useful bits that **protect** them and help them do their job **well**.

Sports use **Lots** of Different **Movement Types**

During exercise, you'll usually use a <u>combination</u> of <u>movement types</u>, and often a combination of <u>joints</u>, either at the same time, or one after another. For example:

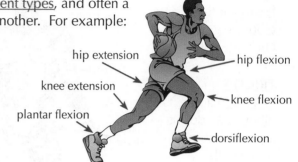

- To do a <u>push-up</u> at the gym or a <u>football throw-in</u>, first you use <u>flexion</u> at the <u>elbow</u> to <u>bend</u> your arms. To <u>straighten</u> your arms again and complete the movements, you <u>extend</u> your arms at the <u>elbow</u>.

- <u>Running</u>, <u>kicking</u>, basic <u>squats</u> and standing vertical <u>jumps</u> all use <u>flexion</u> and <u>extension</u> at the <u>hip</u> and <u>knee</u>. They also use <u>plantar flexion</u> and <u>dorsiflexion</u> at the <u>ankle</u>.

- <u>Bowling</u> in cricket involves the movement of the arm in a <u>circular motion</u> at the <u>shoulder</u>. This action uses <u>circumduction</u> of the shoulder.

hip extension — hip flexion — knee extension — knee flexion — plantar flexion — dorsiflexion

Connective Tissues Join Muscle and Bones

There are <u>three types</u> of <u>connective tissue</u> you need to know about:

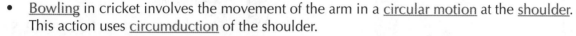

LIGAMENTS — <u>hold bones together</u> to <u>restrict</u> how much joints can move. This helps maintain the <u>stability</u> of the skeleton and prevents <u>dislocation</u> of joints. They're made of <u>tough</u> and <u>fibrous</u> tissue (like very strong <u>string</u>).

Ligaments also protect bones and joints by <u>absorbing shock</u>.

TENDONS — attach <u>muscles</u> to <u>bones</u> (or to other muscles) to allow bones to <u>move</u> when muscles contract.

CARTILAGE — acts as a <u>cushion between bones</u> to prevent <u>damage</u> during joint movement by absorbing shock and preventing friction between bones. It also aids the <u>stability</u> of a joint.

Learn the **Structure** of a **Synovial Joint**

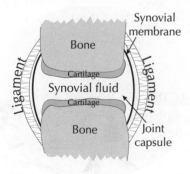

Synovial membrane — Bone — Cartilage — Synovial fluid — Cartilage — Bone — Ligament — Ligament — Joint capsule

<u>Ball and socket</u> and <u>hinge</u> joints are <u>synovial joints</u>. A synovial joint is a joint that allows a <u>wide</u> range of <u>movement</u> and has a <u>joint capsule</u> enclosing and <u>supporting</u> it.

1) The bones at a synovial joint are held together by <u>ligaments</u>.

2) The ends of the bones are covered with <u>cartilage</u> and are shaped so that they <u>fit together</u> and can move <u>smoothly</u>.

3) The <u>synovial membrane</u> releases <u>synovial fluid</u> into the <u>joint capsule</u> to <u>lubricate</u> (or 'oil') the joint, allowing it to <u>move</u> more easily.

4) Most synovial joints also have sacs of fluid called <u>bursae</u> (one is a '<u>bursa</u>') which <u>reduce friction</u> between <u>bones</u> and <u>tissues</u> in and around the joint.

5) This structure helps to <u>prevent injury</u> to the bones that make up your joints.

Two bones working together — it's a joint effort...

Those <u>connective tissues</u> are really important — they all help your performance in physical activity and sport in a different way. Keep revising what each one does so you don't get them mixed up in the exam.

The Muscular System

The **skeleton** needs **muscles** to move the body — together these are known as the **musculo-skeletal system**.

Learn the **Name** and **Function** of These **Muscles**

BICEPS — flexion at the elbow, e.g. when curling weights.

TRICEPS — extension at the elbow, e.g. during a jump shot in basketball.

PECTORALS — adduction and flexion (horizontally) at the shoulder, e.g. during a forehand drive in tennis.

pectorals

deltoids

biceps

hip flexors

abdominals

quadriceps

gluteals

tibialis anterior

gastrocnemius (calf)

rotator cuff

triceps

latissimus dorsi

hamstrings

HAMSTRINGS — flexion at the knee, e.g. bringing the foot back before kicking a football.

QUADRICEPS — extension at the knee, e.g. when performing a drop kick in rugby.

GASTROCNEMIUS — plantar flexion at the ankle, e.g. standing on the toes in ballet pointe work.

HIP FLEXORS — flexion of the leg at the hip, e.g. lifting the knee when sprinting.

DELTOID — flexion, extension, abduction or circumduction at the shoulder. E.g. during front crawl in swimming.

TIBIALIS ANTERIOR — dorsiflexion at the ankle, e.g. during a heel side turn in snowboarding.

ABDOMINALS — flexion at the waist, e.g. during a sit-up.

GLUTEALS — extension, rotation, and abduction of the leg at the hip, e.g. pushing the body forward when running.

LATISSIMUS DORSI — extension, adduction or rotation at the shoulder, e.g. during butterfly stroke in swimming.

ROTATOR CUFFS — rotation and abduction at the shoulder, e.g. lifting the arms when preparing to dive. They also stabilise the shoulder joint during other movements.

There are **Different Types** of **Muscle Contraction**

When a muscle contracts, it creates tension to apply force to a bone.
Muscle contractions can be isometric or isotonic.

ISOMETRIC CONTRACTION
The muscle stays the same length, and so nothing moves.

Like if you pull on a rope attached to a wall.

ISOTONIC CONTRACTION
The muscle changes length and so something moves.

Like if you exercise with weights that are free to move.

There are also two types of isotonic contraction — concentric and eccentric.

CONCENTRIC CONTRACTION
This is when a muscle contracts and shortens. This type of contraction pulls on a bone to cause a movement to happen. E.g. during the upward phase of a biceps curl, your biceps undergoes a concentric contraction to pull your forearm and lift the weight.

ECCENTRIC CONTRACTION
This is when a muscle contracts and lengthens. This helps you to control the speed of a movement. E.g. during the downward phase of a biceps curl, your biceps contracts eccentrically, creating tension so that the weight falls slowly.

The Muscular System

Now on to more stuff about muscles — just what we were all hoping for. This page'll look at how muscles **work together** to produce different movement types at the **joints** in the body.

Antagonistic Muscles Work in **Pairs**

Muscles can only do one thing — <u>pull</u>. To make a joint move in two directions, you need <u>two muscles</u> that can pull in <u>opposite directions</u>.

1) <u>Antagonistic</u> muscles are <u>pairs of muscles</u> that work <u>against</u> each other.
2) One muscle <u>contracts</u> while the other one <u>relaxes</u>, and <u>vice versa</u>.
3) The muscle that's contracting is the <u>agonist</u> or <u>prime mover</u>.
4) The muscle that's relaxing is the <u>antagonist</u>.
5) Each muscle is attached to <u>two</u> bones by <u>tendons</u>.
6) Only <u>one</u> of the bones connected at the joint actually moves.

Here, 'contracts' means 'shortens', and 'relaxes' means 'lengthens'. But you might see 'contracts' used to mean 'creates tension' — which muscles do when they shorten and lengthen (see previous page).

You need to know some **Antagonistic Muscle Pairs**

There are <u>antagonistic muscle pairs</u> at different <u>joints</u> in the body:

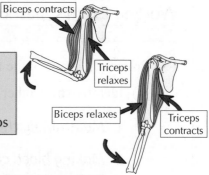

Biceps contracts
Triceps relaxes
Biceps relaxes
Triceps contracts

KNEE

<u>Flexion</u> — <u>agonist</u> — hamstrings
    <u>antagonist</u> — quadriceps
<u>Extension</u> — <u>agonist</u> — quadriceps
    <u>antagonist</u> — hamstrings

ELBOW

<u>Flexion</u> — <u>agonist</u> — biceps
    <u>antagonist</u> — triceps
<u>Extension</u> — <u>agonist</u> — triceps
    <u>antagonist</u> — biceps

HIP

<u>Flexion</u> — <u>agonist</u> — hip flexors
    <u>antagonist</u> — gluteals
<u>Extension</u> — <u>agonist</u> — gluteals
    <u>antagonist</u> — hip flexors

ANKLE

<u>Plantar flexion</u> — <u>agonist</u> — gastrocnemius
    <u>antagonist</u> — tibialis anterior
<u>Dorsiflexion</u> — <u>agonist</u> — tibialis anterior
    <u>antagonist</u> — gastrocnemius

Other muscles are used in these shoulder movements — these are just the <u>main ones</u>.

SHOULDER

<u>Flexion</u> — <u>agonist</u> — front part of deltoid
    <u>antagonist</u> — back part of deltoid
<u>Extension</u> — <u>agonist</u> — back part of deltoid
    <u>antagonist</u> — front part of deltoid

<u>Adduction</u> — <u>agonist</u> — latissimus dorsi
    <u>antagonist</u> — middle part of deltoid
<u>Abduction</u> — <u>agonist</u> — middle part of deltoid
    <u>antagonist</u> — latissimus dorsi

<u>Rotation</u> (turning arm outwards) — <u>agonists</u> — infraspinatus, teres minor
    <u>antagonist</u> — subscapularis
<u>Rotation</u> (turning arm inwards) — <u>agonist</u> — subscapularis
    <u>antagonists</u> — infraspinatus, teres minor

The infraspinatus, teres minor and subscapularis are muscles in the <u>rotator cuffs</u> at the shoulders.

Antagonists — don't let them get to you...

This page might look tricky with all these different antagonistic muscle pairs to learn, but just remember — the muscle that's the <u>agonist</u> in one movement will be the <u>antagonist</u> in the opposite movement.

Warm-Up and Worked Exam Questions

Time for some questions on the skeletal and muscular systems. There are some warm-up questions and worked exam questions to get you started, then some exam questions for you to practice on your own.

Warm-Up Questions

1) What do bones protect — vital organs, muscles or joints?
2) Name a long bone found in the leg and give an example of a sporting movement it is used in.
3) Which joint movement involves closing a joint?
4) Give one example of a ball and socket joint and say what types of joint movement it allows.
5) Name three types of connective tissue.
6) Describe the function of synovial fluid.
7) Which muscle is responsible for plantar flexion at the ankle?
8) What type of muscle contraction happens when a muscle lengthens — concentric or eccentric?
9) What is the name given to a pair of muscles that work against each other?
10) Which pair of muscles work against each other to cause extension at the knee?

Worked Exam Questions

1   Protection is one of the functions of the skeleton.

   (a) Identify **three** other functions of the skeleton. (Grade 1-3)

   1 .Maintaining.the.body's.shape...........................

   2 .Making.blood.cells.......................................

   3 .Allowing.movement.......................................

   > You could also put "mineral storage", but you only need three functions to get the marks.

   [3 marks]

   (b) Using **one** example, suggest how the cranium could protect a performer when taking part in sport. (Grade 3-5)

   .During.a.game.of.hockey,.if.a.player.were.to.be.hit.on.the.head.by.the.ball,...........

   .the.cranium.would.protect.the.brain.from.a.serious.injury.................................

   [1 mark]

2   Identify **one** example of a sporting action that uses abduction of the arm at the shoulder. (Grade 3-5)

   .Preparing.to.swing.a.hockey.stick...

   > You'd get the mark for any example that involves moving the arm away from an imaginary centre line on the body.

   [1 mark]

Exam Questions

1 A ballet dancer performs a movement. She uses her ankle joint to point her toes. (Grade 3-5)

(a) Identify the type of synovial joint working at the ankle.

....

[1 mark]

(b) Outline how **two** features of the ankle joint help the ballet dancer avoid injury.

1 ....

2 ....

[2 marks]

2 **Figure 1** shows a basketball player throwing a ball. (Grade 7-9)

Figure 1

Position **A**   Position **B**

Explain how the muscles and bones work together as the basketball player moves from Position **A** to Position **B**.

....

....

....

....

....

....

[3 marks]

The Cardiovascular System

Your cardiovascular system's job is to **move blood** around your body. As the blood travels around, it does loads of really **useful stuff** to help you **take part** in physical activity and sport. Read on to find out more...

The **Cardiovascular System** has Different Functions

1) The cardiovascular system helps <u>transport</u> things around the body in the bloodstream, like <u>oxygen</u>, <u>carbon dioxide</u>, and <u>nutrients</u> (e.g. glucose).

Have a look at p.18 for more about how muscles use oxygen and glucose.

2) This gives the <u>muscles</u> what they need to <u>release energy</u> to <u>move</u> during exercise (and takes away any <u>waste</u> products).

3) When exercising, more blood is moved nearer to the skin to <u>cool</u> the body more quickly. This means you can exercise for a <u>long time</u> without <u>overheating</u> (see p.20).

Learn How the **Heart Pumps Blood** Around the **Body**

1) The <u>cardiovascular system</u> is made up of three main parts — the <u>heart</u>, <u>blood</u> and <u>blood vessels</u>.

Arteries, veins and capillaries are the main types of blood vessel.

2) During any kind of <u>physical activity</u>, blood needs to <u>circulate</u> around the body to deliver <u>oxygen</u> and <u>glucose</u> to your <u>muscles</u>, and to <u>take carbon dioxide away</u> from them. This is where the <u>heart</u> comes in.

RIGHT SIDE

- <u>Deoxygenated blood</u> enters the <u>right atrium</u> from the <u>vena cava</u> (a <u>vein</u>) as the heart <u>relaxes</u>.
- The right atrium <u>contracts</u>, pushing the blood through a <u>valve</u> into the <u>right ventricle</u>.
- The right ventricle <u>contracts</u>, pushing the blood through another <u>valve</u> into the <u>pulmonary artery</u>, which carries the blood to the <u>lungs</u>.
- Gases are <u>exchanged</u> in the <u>lungs</u> and the blood is <u>oxygenated</u> (see p.14 for more information).

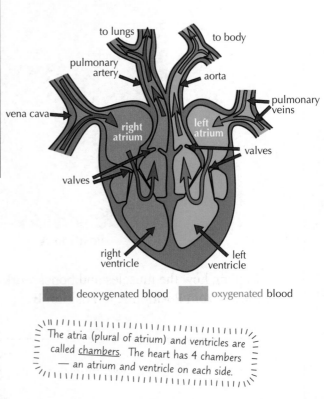

to lungs · to body · pulmonary artery · aorta · pulmonary veins · vena cava · right atrium · left atrium · valves · valves · right ventricle · left ventricle

deoxygenated blood   oxygenated blood

The atria (plural of atrium) and ventricles are called <u>chambers</u>. The heart has 4 chambers — an atrium and ventricle on each side.

LEFT SIDE

- <u>Oxygenated blood</u> enters the <u>left atrium</u> from the <u>pulmonary vein</u> as the heart <u>relaxes</u>.
- The left atrium <u>contracts</u>, pushing the blood through a <u>valve</u> into the <u>left ventricle</u>.
- The left ventricle <u>contracts</u>, pushing the blood through another <u>valve</u> into the <u>aorta</u> (an <u>artery</u>). This transports the <u>oxygenated blood</u> to the rest of the <u>body</u> — including the muscles.
- When the muscles have <u>used</u> the oxygen in the blood, it becomes <u>deoxygenated</u> again.

3) <u>Diastole</u> is when the heart <u>relaxes</u> and <u>fills</u> with blood and <u>systole</u> is when it <u>contracts</u> and <u>pumps</u> the blood out. <u>Both sides</u> of the heart <u>relax</u> at the <u>same time</u> and then <u>contract</u> at the <u>same time</u>. <u>One cardiac cycle</u> is a phase of diastole and systole — it might help to think of this as one 'heartbeat'.

4) Blood <u>flows</u> because of differences in <u>pressure</u> caused by the cardiac cycle. <u>Valves open</u> to let blood <u>fill</u> the heart chambers, and <u>close</u> to <u>prevent backflow</u> — this is when blood flows the wrong way.

Each valve has a name, but you don't need to know them for the exam.

The Cardiovascular System

Your cardiovascular system has different types of **blood vessels** that carry blood around your body. This page'll tell you all about them, as well as some of the wonderful stuff your blood is **made of**.

Arteries, Veins and Capillaries Carry Blood

1) <u>Blood vessels</u> transport <u>blood</u> — they have a hollow centre called the <u>lumen</u> so blood can <u>flow through</u>. The <u>diameter</u> of the lumen <u>varies</u> for the different types of blood vessel.

2) <u>Blood pressure</u> measures <u>how strongly</u> the blood <u>presses</u> against the <u>walls</u> of blood vessels. Blood vessels with <u>thicker walls</u> can carry blood at <u>higher pressure</u>.

3) Different <u>types</u> of blood vessel are suited to <u>different roles</u>:

ARTERIES — carry blood <u>away</u> from the heart. All arteries carry <u>oxygenated blood</u> except for the <u>pulmonary arteries</u>. Their <u>thick</u>, <u>muscular</u> walls allow them to carry blood flowing at <u>high pressure</u>.

The muscle in the walls of arteries and veins allows them to widen and narrow to control blood flow (see p.20).

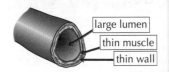

VEINS — carry blood <u>towards</u> the heart. They have <u>valves</u> to stop blood flowing the wrong way. All veins carry <u>deoxygenated blood</u>, except for the <u>pulmonary veins</u>. They carry blood at <u>low pressure</u>, so they have <u>thinner walls</u> and <u>less muscle</u> than arteries.

CAPILLARIES — carry blood through the body to exchange <u>gases</u> and <u>nutrients</u> with the body's tissues. They have <u>very thin walls</u> (just one cell thick) so substances can <u>easily pass through</u>. They're also very <u>narrow</u>, which means <u>lots</u> of them can fit into the body's tissues — giving them a <u>large surface area</u> to let gas exchange happen more easily. It also means that blood can only flow through them <u>slowly</u> — giving <u>more time</u> for gas exchange.

4) There are also two <u>other small types</u> of blood vessel — <u>arterioles</u> (which branch off arteries) and <u>venules</u> (which meet to form veins).

5) <u>Oxygenated blood</u> flows through <u>arteries</u> into <u>arterioles</u>, then into <u>capillaries</u>.

6) After <u>gases</u> have been <u>exchanged</u> between the <u>capillaries</u> and the body tissues, blood is transported from the capillaries into <u>venules</u>, where it flows back into the <u>veins</u>.

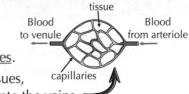
Blood to venule — tissue — Blood from arteriole — capillaries

Your Blood Contains Red and White Blood Cells

You need to know about two types of <u>cells</u> that make up the <u>blood</u> in your body. They have different <u>jobs</u>, which are important in helping your body to take part in <u>physical activity</u>.

RED BLOOD CELLS — Carry <u>oxygen</u> and transport it around the body to be used to release <u>energy</u> needed by <u>muscles</u> during physical activity. They also carry <u>carbon dioxide</u> to the lungs. <u>Haemoglobin</u> (a protein in red blood cells) stores the oxygen and carbon dioxide. <u>Oxyhaemoglobin</u> is formed by oxygen and haemoglobin combining.

See p.20-21 for how the cardiovascular system changes during exercise.

WHITE BLOOD CELLS — Fight <u>against disease</u> so you stay <u>healthy</u> and <u>perform</u> well.

REVISION TIP

Each type of blood vessel has a different job...

If you're struggling to remember whether <u>veins</u> and <u>arteries</u> carry blood to or from the heart, just remember — arteries carry blood <u>away</u> from the heart, so veins must carry blood <u>towards</u> it.

Section One — Anatomy and Physiology

The Respiratory System

You'll probably recognise most of this stuff from **biology** — but there's no harm in a **quick recap**.

Learn the **Structure** of the **Respiratory System**

The respiratory system is <u>everything</u> you use to <u>breathe</u>.
It's found in the <u>chest cavity</u> — the area inside the chest.

TRACHEA

↓

BRONCHI

↓

BRONCHIOLES

↓

ALVEOLI

1) Air passes through the nose or mouth and then on to the <u>trachea</u>.

2) The trachea splits into two tubes called <u>bronchi</u> (each one is a '<u>bronchus</u>') — one going to each <u>lung</u>.

3) The bronchi split into progressively smaller tubes called <u>bronchioles</u>.

4) The bronchioles finally end at small bags called <u>alveoli</u> (each one is an '<u>alveolus</u>') where <u>gases</u> are <u>exchanged</u> (see below).

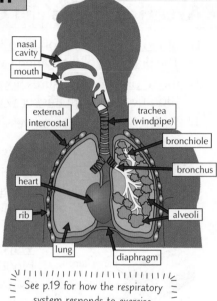

See p.19 for how the respiratory system responds to exercise.

The <u>diaphragm</u> and <u>external intercostal muscles</u> help the air to <u>move</u>:

- When you breathe <u>in</u>, the <u>diaphragm</u> and <u>external intercostals</u> contract to move the <u>ribcage</u> upwards and <u>expand</u> the chest cavity. This <u>decreases</u> the <u>air pressure</u> in the lungs, drawing air in.
- When you breathe <u>out</u>, the <u>diaphragm</u> and the <u>external intercostals</u> relax, moving the <u>ribcage</u> down and <u>shrinking</u> the chest cavity. <u>Air pressure</u> in the lungs <u>increases</u>, forcing air <u>out</u> of the lungs the <u>same way</u> it came in.

Oxygen and **Carbon Dioxide** are **Exchanged** in the Alveoli

- The cardiovascular and respiratory systems have to <u>work together</u> to get <u>oxygen</u> to the muscles, and <u>carbon dioxide</u> away from them. They do this by <u>exchanging</u> gases between the <u>alveoli</u> and <u>capillaries</u> surrounding them.

The cardiovascular and respiratory systems together make up the <u>cardio-respiratory system</u>.

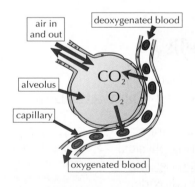

1) <u>Oxygenated blood</u> delivers <u>oxygen</u> and collects <u>carbon dioxide</u> as it <u>circulates</u> around the body. <u>Deoxygenated blood</u> returns to the <u>heart</u> and is then <u>pumped</u> to the <u>lungs</u>.

2) In the lungs, <u>carbon dioxide</u> moves from the blood in the capillaries into the <u>alveoli</u> so it can be <u>breathed out</u>.

3) <u>Oxygen</u> from the <u>air</u> you breathe into the lungs moves across from the alveoli to the <u>red blood cells</u> in the capillaries.

4) The <u>oxygenated blood</u> returns to the <u>heart</u> and is <u>pumped</u> to the rest of the body. The red blood cells <u>carry</u> the oxygen around the body and <u>deliver</u> it where it's needed, e.g. the muscles.

- Alveoli are surrounded by lots of <u>capillaries</u>, giving them a <u>large blood supply</u> to exchange gases with.
- They also have a <u>large surface area</u> and <u>moist</u>, <u>thin walls</u> — so gases only have a <u>short distance</u> to move.
- This <u>exchange</u> of gases happens through a process called <u>diffusion</u>. This means the gases move down a <u>concentration gradient</u> — from a place of <u>higher concentration</u> to a place of <u>lower concentration</u>:

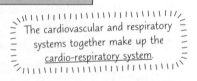

IN ALVEOLUS		IN CAPILLARY
High concentration of O_2 Low concentration of CO_2	DIFFUSION OF O_2 → ← DIFFUSION OF CO_2	Low concentration of O_2 High concentration of CO_2

*O_2 = oxygen
CO_2 = carbon dioxide*

The Respiratory System

The amount of air in your **lungs** can be measured by a snazzy machine called a **spirometer**.

Tidal Volume Increases during Exercise

- The <u>amount of air</u> you breathe in or out during <u>one breath</u> is known as your <u>tidal volume</u>.
  During <u>exercise</u> your tidal volume <u>increases</u> as you take <u>deeper breaths</u> (see p.19).

- After a <u>normal breath in</u>, you can still breathe in <u>more air</u> —
  this extra volume of air is your <u>inspiratory reserve volume</u> (IRV).

- You can also breathe out <u>more air</u> after a <u>normal breath out</u> —
  the extra air you can breathe out is your <u>expiratory reserve volume</u> (ERV).

- After you've <u>breathed out</u> as much air as you can, there's still some
  air <u>left</u> in your lungs. This is called the <u>residual volume</u>.

A Spirometer Trace shows Lung Air Volumes

A <u>spirometer</u> produces a graph called a <u>spirometer trace</u>, which shows the <u>volume of air</u> in your lungs.

This shows one <u>whole breath</u> in and out. The parts of the trace that go <u>up</u> are during <u>inhalation</u>. The parts that go <u>down</u> are during <u>exhalation</u>.

These <u>big changes</u> in volume show a <u>maximum inspiration</u> and <u>maximum expiration</u> — breathing in and out <u>as much as possible</u>.

The <u>small changes</u> in volume show <u>normal breaths</u> in and out.

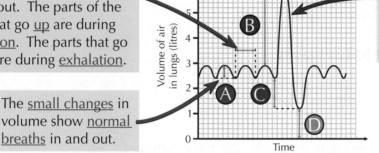

Your IRV and ERV decrease during exercise — you're breathing in and out more air than normal, so you can't breathe in or out as much extra air.

You need to be able to read some <u>lung volumes</u> from a spirometer trace:

A The difference in volume between a 'peak' and a 'dip' shows the <u>tidal volume</u>. When you're not exercising, an <u>average</u> tidal volume is about <u>500 ml</u>.

B The difference in volume here is the <u>inspiratory reserve volume</u>. It's usually about <u>3 litres</u> when you're not exercising.

C This difference in volume gives the <u>expiratory reserve volume</u>. This is usually about <u>1.2 litres</u> when you're at rest.

D This shows the <u>residual volume</u>. It's normally around <u>1.2 litres</u> — both <u>at rest</u> and <u>during exercise</u>.

A spirometer trace can show you whether the person breathing into it was <u>resting</u> or <u>exercising</u>.

1) When you exercise, your <u>tidal volume increases</u> — you take deeper breaths in and out. So during the '<u>exercise</u>' part of the spirometer trace, the 'peaks' are <u>higher</u> and the 'dips' are <u>lower</u> than during the '<u>rest</u>' part.

2) Your <u>breathing rate</u> also increases when you exercise — you take <u>more breaths</u> per minute than when you're resting. This is shown on the spirometer trace by the 'peaks' being <u>closer together</u> during exercise.

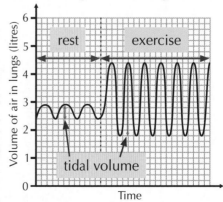

 A spirometer trace changes when exercise starts...

You might need to draw a <u>spirometer trace</u> on a set of axes in your exam. But don't panic if you do — just remember that the 'peaks' of the trace get taller and closer together during exercise.

Warm-Up and Worked Exam Questions

Before you try the cardiovascular and respiratory system exam questions on the next page, warm up with these quick questions and make sure you can follow the answers to the exam questions below.

Warm-Up Questions

1) Name the four chambers of the heart.
2) Which of the following describes when the heart relaxes and fills with blood: diastole or systole?
3) Which type of blood vessel carries blood away from the heart?
4) Which type of blood cell carries oxygen around the body — red or white?
5) Which component of the respiratory system does air pass through next after the nose or mouth?
6) What is meant by residual volume?

Worked Exam Questions

1 State **one** function of capillaries. Grade 1-3

They carry blood to the body's tissues.

Capillaries also exchange gases, transfer nutrients and remove waste products from the body's tissues.

[1 mark]

2 Describe the action of the diaphragm when inhaling and exhaling. Grade 3-5

During inhalation, the diaphragm contracts to expand the chest cavity and draw

air into the lungs. During exhalation, it relaxes into its normal shape, shrinking

the chest cavity and forcing air back out of the lungs.

[2 marks]

3 **Figure 1** shows part of a spirometer trace when the subject was at rest. Grade 3-5

Complete the spirometer trace in **Figure 1** to show the trace during exercise.

Figure 1

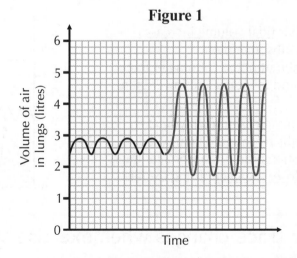

[1 mark]

Exam Questions

1   Which **one** of these is the component of the respiratory system
    where oxygen and carbon dioxide are exchanged?

    Grade 1-3

    Shade **one** oval only.

    A   Bronchioles   ◯
    B   External intercostals   ◯
    C   Diaphragm   ◯
    D   Alveoli   ◯

    [1 mark]

2   Explain **one** way that the structure of arteries makes them suited to their function.

    Grade 3-5

    ....

    ....

    ....

    [2 marks]

3   A performer's breathing changes during exercise.

    Grade 3-5

    (a) Define tidal volume **and** inspiratory reserve volume.

    ....

    ....

    ....

    ....

    [2 marks]

    (b) Outline what happens to tidal volume **and** inspiratory reserve volume during exercise.

    ....

    ....

    [2 marks]

4   Explain why a marathon runner would benefit
    from having a high number of red blood cells.

    Grade 5-7

    ....

    ....

    ....

    ....

    ....

    [3 marks]

Aerobic and Anaerobic Exercise

Your body can release energy in different ways — it all depends on **how hard** and **how long** you're exercising. And different **sources of fuel** can be used to release energy in the muscles. Fantastic stuff.

Aerobic Exercise — With Oxygen

- All the living cells in your body need energy. Normally the body uses oxygen to release energy from glucose (a sugar found in food). This is called aerobic respiration.

> **Glucose + Oxygen → Carbon dioxide + Water + Energy**

Carbon dioxide and water are by-products of aerobic respiration.

- If your body's keeping up with the oxygen demand of its cells, it means there's enough oxygen available for aerobic respiration.
- Exercise where your body can keep up with oxygen demand is called aerobic.

AEROBIC EXERCISE is exercise in the presence of or using oxygen.

- When exercise is not too fast and is steady, the heart can supply all the oxygen that the working muscles need.
- You breathe out the carbon dioxide through your lungs, while the water is lost as sweat, urine, or in the air you breathe out.
- As long as your muscles are supplied with enough oxygen, you can do aerobic exercise — so if you're exercising for long periods, you'll be producing your energy aerobically.
- Aerobic respiration is how marathon runners get their energy — it's the most efficient way to get it.

Anaerobic Exercise — Without Oxygen

1) During vigorous exercise, your body can't supply all the oxygen needed. When this happens, your muscles release energy without using oxygen in a different process called anaerobic respiration.

> **Glucose → Energy + Lactic acid**

Lactic acid is a by-product of anaerobic respiration — you need oxygen to remove it (see next page).

2) Exercise where your body has to do this is called anaerobic.

ANAEROBIC EXERCISE is exercise in the absence of enough oxygen, or without oxygen.

3) When exercise duration is short and at high intensity, the heart and lungs can't supply blood and oxygen to muscles as fast as the cells need them.

4) The lack of oxygen during anaerobic respiration means it can only provide energy for short periods of time — so you can't exercise at high intensity for very long.

5) Sprinters get their energy anaerobically — they have to run quickly for short durations.

Carbohydrates and Fats are used as Fuel

1) Your body needs a source of fuel so that respiration can provide energy.

2) Carbohydrates (from foods such as pasta) and fats stored in the body can both be used as fuel.

CARBOHYDRATES — the body's main source of fuel. They're used during aerobic exercise at moderate intensity and for high intensity anaerobic exercise.

FATS — used as fuel for aerobic exercise at low intensity. Fats provide more energy than carbohydrates, but they can't be used as fuel for higher intensity exercise.

Both types of respiration use glucose to release energy...

Learning some Greek might help you to remember about respiration. 'Aero' translates as air, which contains oxygen, and 'an' means without — so anaerobic respiration is without oxygen.

Short-Term Effects of Exercise

Exercise has loads of different **short-term effects** on the body — some that **help** you to exercise, and others that are just a bit nasty. This page'll look at the effects on your **muscles** and your **breathing**.

There are **Short-Term** Effects on the **Muscular** System

There are loads of different effects on your muscles <u>during exercise</u>, and <u>straight after</u> it.

1) When you exercise, your muscles release <u>extra energy</u> for movement. Producing this energy also <u>generates heat</u>, which can make you feel <u>hot</u> and <u>sweaty</u>.

2) Also, during <u>anaerobic</u> exercise, your muscles produce <u>lactic acid</u>. If you use your muscles <u>anaerobically</u> for too long, the lactic acid starts to <u>build up</u>. This leads to a rise in the <u>lactate levels</u> in the body — <u>lactate accumulation</u>.

3) Lactic acid build-up makes your muscles <u>painful</u> and causes <u>muscle fatigue</u> (tiredness).

4) If your muscles are <u>fatigued</u>, they need <u>oxygen</u> to <u>remove the lactic acid</u> and <u>recover</u>. The amount of <u>oxygen</u> you need is the <u>oxygen debt</u>, or '<u>EPOC</u>' — excess post-exercise oxygen consumption.

5) To <u>repay oxygen debt</u>, you'll need to <u>slow down</u> or <u>stop</u> the exercise you're doing for a while, which can have a <u>negative</u> impact on your <u>performance</u>.

6) During a training session where you do <u>anaerobic exercise</u>, you'll need to have periods of <u>rest</u> or <u>low intensity</u> exercise before you can work anaerobically again.

Working your muscles <u>really hard</u> during a workout can also affect your body <u>a day or two</u> after exercise.

1) You might feel <u>tired</u> because your muscles used up lots of <u>energy</u> during your workout.

A cool-down (see p.54) can help prevent these effects.

2) You could also feel <u>sick</u> and <u>light-headed</u>.

3) Some people get '<u>delayed onset of muscle soreness</u>' (DOMS), or <u>muscle cramp</u>.

There are **Short-Term** Effects on the **Respiratory** System

- During exercise, <u>muscles</u> such as the <u>pectorals</u> and the <u>sternocleidomastoid</u> (in the neck) <u>expand</u> your lungs more to let in <u>extra air</u>. Muscles in your <u>abdomen</u> also work to pull your <u>ribcage</u> down and shrink the chest cavity quicker, so you <u>breathe out</u> faster.

- These changes help to increase your <u>depth of breathing</u> (which leads to an increase in your <u>tidal volume</u> — see p.15) and <u>rate</u> of <u>breathing</u> (the <u>number of breaths</u> per minute).

- This means <u>more oxygen</u> is taken in and transferred to the blood, which helps to meet the <u>increased demand</u> for oxygen in the <u>muscles</u> during physical activity.

- It also helps you to <u>breathe out</u> the extra <u>carbon dioxide</u> produced during aerobic respiration.

- These changes allow you to do <u>aerobic exercise</u> for <u>long periods</u> of time.

- If you've been doing <u>anaerobic exercise</u>, your breathing rate and depth will remain higher than normal until you've taken in enough <u>oxygen</u> to 'pay off' your <u>oxygen debt</u>.

These changes to your respiratory system will all be <u>more extreme</u> if you exercise really <u>intensely</u>. So you'll breathe <u>deeper</u> and <u>quicker</u> when you're exercising <u>hard</u> than when you're doing <u>light exercise</u>.

Brain fatigue — a short-term effect of PE revision...

It's not enough just knowing that you breathe faster and deeper during exercise — you need to know why, too. So remember, you need to get <u>extra oxygen</u> into the lungs, and <u>extra carbon dioxide</u> out of them.

Short-Term Effects of Exercise

Your **cardiovascular system** works extra **hard** during exercise to make sure your **muscles** get what they need to work properly. This includes using your **blood vessels** to send your **blood** where it's needed the most.

There are **Short-Term** Effects on the **Cardiovascular** System

1) Your heart rate is the number of times your heart beats per minute. An adult's resting heart rate (their heart rate when they aren't exercising) is usually about 60-80 bpm (beats per minute).

2) Your stroke volume is the amount of blood each ventricle pumps with each contraction (or heartbeat).

3) During exercise, your heart rate and stroke volume both increase.

4) This leads to an increase in your cardiac output — the volume of blood pumped by a ventricle per minute.

> cardiac output (Q) = heart rate × stroke volume

5) It also increases the pressure of your blood as your heart beats — your systolic blood pressure.

> Diastolic blood pressure is your blood's pressure when your heart is relaxed. It doesn't change much during exercise.

6) An increase in cardiac output increases the blood and oxygen supply to your muscles — so they can release the energy they need for physical activity. It also removes more carbon dioxide from the muscles and takes it to the lungs to be breathed out.

7) Your heart rate, stroke volume and cardiac output will remain higher than normal after exercise until any oxygen debt is paid off.

> The harder you're exercising, the higher your heart rate, stroke volume and cardiac output will be. So if you're only doing very light exercise, they'll be lower than if you were doing really strenuous exercise.

Your Blood Vessels **Change** when you **Exercise**

When you exercise, blood is redistributed around the body to increase the supply of oxygen to your muscles.

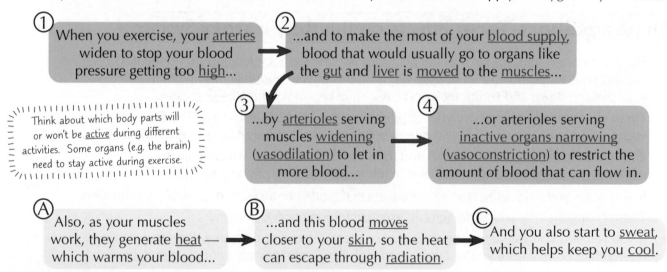

① When you exercise, your arteries widen to stop your blood pressure getting too high...

② ...and to make the most of your blood supply, blood that would usually go to organs like the gut and liver is moved to the muscles...

> Think about which body parts will or won't be active during different activities. Some organs (e.g. the brain) need to stay active during exercise.

③ ...by arterioles serving muscles widening (vasodilation) to let in more blood...

④ ...or arterioles serving inactive organs narrowing (vasoconstriction) to restrict the amount of blood that can flow in.

Ⓐ Also, as your muscles work, they generate heat — which warms your blood...

Ⓑ ...and this blood moves closer to your skin, so the heat can escape through radiation.

Ⓒ And you also start to sweat, which helps keep you cool.

The amount of blood that's redistributed depends on how intensely you're exercising. So during light exercise, only a small amount of blood is moved towards your working muscles. But if you're exercising really hard, a lot more blood is moved.

Give your brain a quick exercise — learn this page...

Remember, blood is redistributed during exercise because your muscles need more oxygen than some of your organs do. And this couldn't happen without vasodilation and vasoconstriction of blood vessels.

Short-Term Effects of Exercise

This page'll show you how the **cardiovascular** and **respiratory** systems **team up** to help you exercise. It'll also give you some handy tips on how to **interpret heart rate data** that you might see in the exam.

The **Cardiovascular** and **Respiratory** Systems Work **Together**

1) During exercise (and immediately after), <u>more oxygen</u> is delivered to the muscles than normal. Extra <u>carbon dioxide</u> is also taken away from them and <u>breathed out</u>.

2) The <u>cardiovascular</u> and <u>respiratory</u> systems work together to make this happen. When you exercise:

MORE O₂ DELIVERED

- <u>Breathing rate</u> and <u>depth</u> increase, so more oxygen is delivered to the <u>alveoli</u> in the lungs.
- <u>Cardiac output</u> also increases — so <u>blood</u> passes through the lungs at a <u>faster rate</u>, and picks up the <u>extra oxygen</u> from the <u>alveoli</u>. It's then delivered to the <u>muscles</u>.

MORE CO₂ REMOVED

- Increased <u>cardiac output</u> means that the blood can transport <u>carbon dioxide</u> from the <u>muscles</u> to the <u>lungs</u> more <u>quickly</u>.
- Here it moves back into the <u>alveoli</u>, and the higher <u>breathing rate</u> and <u>depth</u> allow it to be quickly <u>breathed out</u>.

3) These changes maintain a <u>high concentration gradient</u> — after you breathe in, there's a lot <u>more oxygen</u> in the <u>alveoli</u> than the capillaries, and a lot <u>more carbon dioxide</u> in the <u>capillaries</u> than the alveoli.

4) This allows <u>diffusion</u> of the gases to happen <u>much quicker</u> during exercise.

5) These processes help you to release enough <u>energy</u> to <u>exercise</u> aerobically and to <u>recover</u> from <u>oxygen debt</u> after anaerobic exercise (see p.19).

For more on diffusion, have a look at page 14.

Heart Rate can be shown Graphically

- In your exam, you might get a <u>graph</u> showing a person's <u>heart rate</u> during a workout.
- This <u>increases</u> during exercise, and gradually goes <u>back to normal</u> once they stop exercising.
- You can use this fact to <u>interpret</u> data and work out whether the person was <u>resting</u>, <u>exercising</u> or <u>recovering</u> at a specific time.

Your <u>heart rate</u> might go up slightly just <u>before</u> you start exercising — this is known as an <u>anticipatory rise</u>.

(A) This point is <u>before</u> the person has started exercising. Their heart rate is at its <u>lowest point</u> — it's their <u>resting heart rate</u>.

(B) Their heart rate has started to <u>increase</u> — they've started to exercise.

(C) Their heart rate reaches <u>130 bpm</u> and <u>stays the same</u> for five minutes — they exercise at the <u>same intensity</u> for that time.

(D) This part of the graph is when the workout is at its <u>highest intensity</u>. The person's heart rate is at its <u>highest</u> point on the graph.

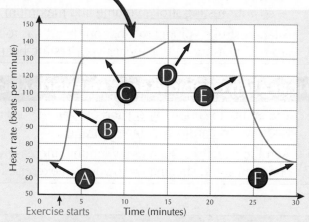

(E) Their heart rate is <u>decreasing</u> — exercise has <u>stopped</u>, or they're completing a <u>cool down</u>. Their heart rate <u>stays fairly high</u> for a while to help with <u>recovery</u>.

(F) They've returned to their <u>resting</u> heart rate of 70 beats per minute.

Interpreting graphs — this doesn't sound like PE...

If you get given a question about <u>heart rate data</u> in your exam, just remember that heart rate <u>goes up</u> during exercise, and comes back <u>down</u> afterwards. Then you can use that fact to work out what was going on at a certain time when a value was recorded.

Long-Term Effects of Exercise

Exercising regularly eventually leads to loads of adaptations in the body's systems.
These benefit your health and different components of fitness, which will help improve your performance.

Exercise Improves the Musculo-Skeletal System

Long-term effects of exercise can take months or years to become noticeable.
There are lots of ways that regular exercise can benefit your musculo-skeletal system:

MUSCLE HYPERTROPHY

1) Doing regular exercise will make your muscles thicker and reduce the weight of your body (by using fat to supply glucose). This can change your body shape.

2) This thickening of muscles is called hypertrophy. It happens to all muscles when they're exercised, including your heart.

3) The thicker a muscle is, the more strongly it can contract — so this increases your strength.

4) Hypertrophy also improves your muscular endurance — so you can use your muscles for longer.

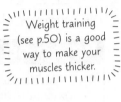
Weight training (see p.50) is a good way to make your muscles thicker.

See p.89-90 for more about the long-term benefits of exercise.

STRONGER LIGAMENTS & TENDONS

Having stronger ligaments and tendons means you're less likely to injure yourself, e.g. dislocation.
Repeated use of muscles and joints can increase suppleness.

INCREASED SPEED

Over long periods of time, intense anaerobic exercises, such as sprinting, can improve your speed, as well as help you recover more quickly after exercise.

Exercise Improves the Cardio-Respiratory System

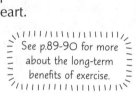
Training that involves aerobic exercise works best to improve the cardio-respiratory system.

BIGGER/STRONGER HEART

- Your heart is just a muscle — when you exercise, it adapts and gets bigger and stronger. This is called cardiac hypertrophy.

- A bigger, stronger heart will contract more strongly and pump more blood with each beat — so your resting stroke volume and maximum cardiac output will increase.

- A larger stroke volume means your heart has to beat less often to pump the same amount of blood around your body. This means your resting heart rate decreases — which is called bradycardia.

INCREASED CARDIOVASCULAR ENDURANCE / STAMINA

- The ability to supply blood and oxygen to your muscles is known as cardiovascular endurance.

- Aerobic exercises, such as swimming, increase your cardiovascular endurance and stamina — so you can exercise for longer.

There's more about cardiovascular endurance on p.33.

Exercise can Improve Components of Fitness

You can target specific areas of fitness (see pages 33-36) to improve, for example:

- A gymnast could increase their suppleness, so they can perform more difficult skills (e.g. a split jump).
- A cyclist could increase their cardiovascular endurance, so they have the stamina to cycle long distances.

Breaking news — exercise is good for you...

To get all these effects, you need to rest after exercise to recover and let your body adapt to any changes.

Warm-Up and Worked Exam Questions

That's the types and effects of exercise all done. These warm-up questions will make sure you've got the basics, then you can look at the exam answers below and try some exam questions for yourself.

Warm-Up Questions

1) Which type of exercise uses oxygen — aerobic or anaerobic?
2) Name one waste product produced during aerobic exercise.
3) What is 'oxygen debt'?
4) What effect does exercise have on your breathing rate?
5) What happens to your stroke volume when you exercise?
6) How could you calculate your cardiac output?
7) Give one example of a long-term effect of exercise on the musculo-skeletal system.
8) What is 'cardiac hypertrophy'?

Worked Exam Questions

1 State **one** short-term effect of exercise on the cardiovascular system. (Grade 1-3)

Increased heart rate. ←

There are other possible answers here. For example, you might have said increased blood pressure or cardiac output.

[1 mark]

2 One long-term effect of exercise can be an increase in muscle strength. (Grade 5-7)

Explain, using **one** example, how this could benefit performance in physical activity and sport.

An increase in muscle strength means that a performer can use more force in their actions. This would benefit a rugby player during a tackle, as it would help them to pull an opponent to the ground.

[3 marks]

3 Hitesh has been training for a marathon for six months. During this time, he has noticed a decrease in his resting heart rate. (Grade 7-9)

Explain how Hitesh's marathon training will have led to a decrease in his resting heart rate.

Think about the effects on the heart <u>during</u> a marathon training session, and the effect this would have in the <u>long term</u>.

Running is aerobic exercise which causes the heart to work harder, which leads to muscle hypertrophy of the heart in the long term. This increases resting stroke volume and therefore decreases resting heart rate, as the heart can deliver the same amount of blood to the rest of the body with fewer beats.

[4 marks]

Exam Questions

1 Which **one** of these effects of exercise could occur 24 to 36 hours after exercise?

Shade **one** oval only.

A   Increase in heart rate   ◯

B   Change in body shape   ◯

C   Delayed onset of muscle soreness   ◯

D   Increase in tidal volume   ◯

[1 mark]

2 **Figure 1** shows the heart rate of a performer during workout A.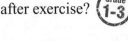

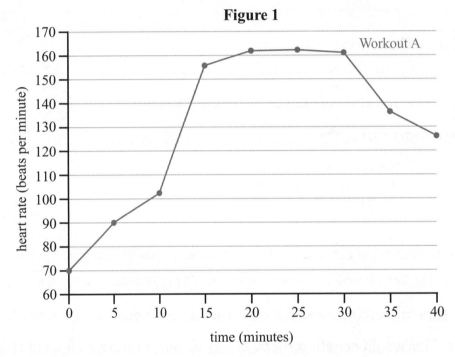

Figure 1

(a) Plot the data shown in **Table 1** on **Figure 1** above. Join up the points to make a line graph.

Table 1 — heart rate of the performer during workout B

Time (minutes)	0	5	10	15	20	25	30	35	40
Heart rate (bpm)	70	80	90	115	130	135	135	120	110

[1 mark]

(b) Analyse the heart rate data in **Figure 1** to explain what it suggests about the difference in intensity between workout A and workout B.

....

....

....

[2 marks]

Exam Questions

3   Blood can be redistributed around the body to meet the demands of physical activity.   (Grade 5-7)

Identify **one** area of the body that would experience an increase in blood flow when swimming. Justify your choice.

....

....

....

....

[3 marks]

4   Outline what aerobic and anaerobic respiration are, and evaluate the importance of these types of respiration during a 50-mile cycling race.

> These 9-markers can look scary, but you'll pick up marks for definitions and examples.

....

....

....

....

....

....

....

....

....

....

....

....

....

....

....

....

....

....

[9 marks]

Revision Summary

Knowledge
Organiser

Quick
Quiz

Let's see how much Anatomy and Physiology you've inhaled. There's lots to learn here, so:

*   Use the **Knowledge Organiser** to go over all the **key points**.
*   Try an **online quiz** for a quick bit of **extra practice** on Sections One and Two.
*   Tackle the **summary questions** below. Yes, they're hard — try to answer them **from memory** to **really test** how well you know the topic. The **answers** are all **in the section**, so go over anything **you're unsure of** again.

The Musculo-Skeletal System (p.4-9) ☑

1)   Describe the five main functions of the skeleton.

2)   The three main types of bone in the body are long bones, short bones and flat bones. What is the function of each type of bone?

3)   a)   Draw a table with three columns, one for each type of bone — long, short and flat. In each column, list as many examples of that type of bone as you can and state their location in the body.
     b)   Can you think of any other bones that don't fit into those three columns? Where are they found?

4)   Name eight different types of joint movement. Can you draw a simple diagram illustrating each one?

5)   For each of the following joints, say what type of joint it is and what type of movement it allows:
     a)   shoulder   b)   elbow   c)   hip   d)   knee   e)   ankle

6)   Describe the function of: a)   cartilage   b)   ligaments   c)   tendons

7)   Sketch a simple diagram of a synovial joint. Add labels to your diagram naming each structure and describing how they each help to prevent injury.

8)   Give the location and function of these muscles:
     a)   pectorals   b)   abdominals   c)   latissimus dorsi   d)   deltoid   e)   rotator cuffs

9)   What is the difference between an isometric and an isotonic muscle contraction?

10) Describe how antagonistic muscle pairs work together.

11) Which two muscles make up the antagonistic muscle pair operating at the:
     a)   elbow joint?   b)   knee joint?   c)   hip?   d)   ankle?
     For bonus points, say which muscle is the agonist and which is the antagonist for flexion.

The Cardio-Respiratory System and Respiration (p.12-15) ☑

12) Describe the pathway of the blood in: a)   the left side of the heart.   b)   the right side of the heart. Try to include the phrases 'oxygenated/deoxygenated blood', 'systole' and 'diastole'.

13) List the three types of blood vessel found in the body. What are their main functions? How are they adapted for those functions?

14) What is the function of red blood cells?

15) List the structures air passes though after it enters the mouth or nose.

16) Describe the process of breathing in. And now breathing out.

17) How are alveoli adapted for efficient gas exchange?

18) What is meant by tidal volume?

19) What are the lung volumes labelled A-D on this spirometer trace? ➡

Aerobic and Anaerobic Exercise and The Effects of Exercise (p.18-22) ☑

20) Explain the differences between aerobic and anaerobic respiration. In what type of exercise would your body use anaerobic respiration?

21) What is EPOC?

22) Describe three ways you might not feel great a day or so after doing some really intense exercise.

23) Explain why your depth and rate of breathing increase during exercise.

24) Why do heart rate, stroke volume and cardiac output remain higher after exercise?

25) Explain what vasodilation and vasoconstriction are and why they happen during exercise.

26) How does regular exercise benefit the ligaments and tendons?

27) Give two long-term effects of exercise on the cardiovascular system.

Lever Systems

When the **muscular** and **skeletal systems** work together, they create **lever systems** that help us to **move**.

Lever Systems Help the Body to Move

A <u>lever</u> is a <u>rigid bar</u> that moves about a <u>fixed point</u> when <u>force</u> is applied to it.
When a <u>muscle</u> pulls on a <u>bone</u> to move a body part about a <u>joint</u>, it uses the body part as a <u>lever</u>.
This lever makes up part of a <u>lever system</u> that has <u>four</u> different components:

1) The <u>lever arm</u> — the <u>bone</u> or <u>body part</u> being moved about a point.
   On a diagram of a lever system, it's shown as a <u>straight line</u>.
2) The <u>fulcrum</u> — the <u>joint</u> where the lever arm <u>pivots</u>. It's shown as a <u>triangle</u>.
3) The <u>effort</u> — the <u>force</u> applied by the <u>muscles</u> to the lever arm.
   It's shown by an <u>arrow</u> pointing in the direction of the force.
4) The <u>load</u> or <u>resistance</u> against the pull of the muscles on the lever arm.
   E.g. the weight of the body, or body part, or something being lifted.
   A <u>square</u> or an <u>arrow</u> is used to represent the load.

You might be asked to draw a diagram of a lever system used in a sporting movement — make sure you label the fulcrum, effort and load (see below).

Levers can be **First**, **Second** or **Third Class**

First Class Levers

First Class — The <u>load</u> and <u>effort</u> are at <u>opposite ends</u> of the lever. The fulcrum is in the middle.

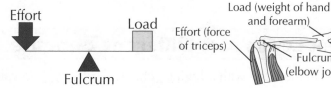

First class levers are used in <u>elbow extension</u>. E.g. for a football throw-in.

Second Class Levers

Second Class — The <u>fulcrum</u> and <u>effort</u> are at <u>opposite ends</u> of the lever. The load is in the middle.

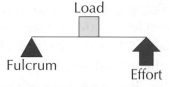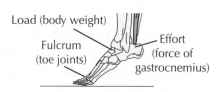

Second class levers are used in <u>plantar flexion</u> and <u>dorsiflexion</u> at the ankle while <u>standing</u>. E.g. when you stand on your toes to <u>jump</u>.

Third Class Levers

Third Class — The <u>fulcrum</u> and <u>load</u> are at <u>opposite ends</u> of the lever. The effort is in the middle.

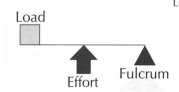

Third class levers are used in <u>elbow flexion</u> (e.g. lifting a weight) and in <u>flexion</u> and <u>extension</u> at the <u>shoulder</u>, <u>hip</u> and <u>knee</u>.

Lever class depends on the order of components...

You can tell the class of a lever by its middle component. So to remember which class is which, use '1, 2, 3, F, L, E'. The letters tell you the middle component of each lever — for first class levers it's the <u>f</u>ulcrum, for second class levers it's the <u>l</u>oad, and for third class levers it's the <u>e</u>ffort.

Lever Systems

Levers **help** the body use its muscles **effectively**. Different levers have **different benefits** — some help to move **heavier loads**, while others increase the **speed** a load can be moved at, or the **range of movement**.

Levers have a **Mechanical Advantage**

1) In a lever system, the <u>distance</u> between the <u>fulcrum</u> and the <u>effort</u> is called the <u>effort arm</u>, and the <u>distance</u> between the <u>fulcrum</u> and the <u>load</u> is called the <u>weight (resistance) arm</u>.

2) You need to be able to <u>label</u> the effort arm and weight arm on a <u>diagram</u> of a lever system. Here's an example of a second class lever with the correct labels:

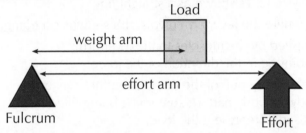

3) The <u>mechanical advantage</u> of a lever depends on the <u>effort arm</u> and the <u>weight arm</u>:

<u>Mechanical advantage</u> = effort arm ÷ weight (resistance) arm

4) The <u>value</u> of the <u>mechanical advantage</u> tells you about the <u>benefits</u> of the lever (see below).

Different Levers have **Different Benefits**

- A lever in the body with a <u>high mechanical advantage</u> (a value <u>bigger</u> than 1) can move a <u>large load</u> with a <u>small effort</u> from the muscles. However, it can only move the load <u>short distances</u> at <u>low speeds</u>.

- <u>Second class</u> levers have a <u>high mechanical advantage</u> — the <u>effort arm</u> is longer than the <u>weight arm</u>.

> E.g. the second class lever used at the ankle when you stand on your toes has a high mechanical advantage. There is only a small effort from your gastrocnemius, but it moves a large load (your whole body weight).

- A lever with a <u>low mechanical advantage</u> (a value <u>less</u> than 1) requires a <u>large effort</u> from the muscles to move a <u>small load</u> — but it can move the load <u>quickly</u> through a <u>large range of movement</u>.

- <u>Third class levers</u> have a <u>low mechanical advantage</u> — the <u>effort arm</u> is shorter than the <u>weight arm</u>.

- A <u>first class lever</u> can have a <u>high or low</u> mechanical advantage:

A <u>first class lever</u> will have a <u>high</u> mechanical advantage if the <u>fulcrum</u> is closer to the <u>load</u> than it is to the <u>effort</u>.

A <u>first class lever</u> will have a <u>low</u> mechanical advantage if the <u>fulcrum</u> is closer to the <u>effort</u> than it is to the <u>load</u>.

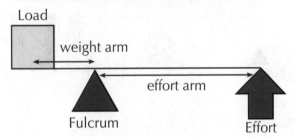

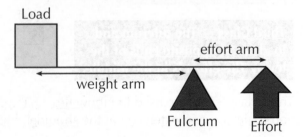

Give it your best effort to learn this page...

'Low' mechanical advantage makes it sound like third class levers aren't as useful as second class levers. So don't forget, levers only have a low mechanical advantage because they're not very good at moving heavy loads — but they're great at moving quickly and through a large range of movement.

Planes and Axes of Movement

It might seem strange that there's a page about planes and axes in a PE book — but it'll all make sense soon. Basically, you can describe a body movement using the **plane** it **moves in** and the **axis** it **moves around**.

Movements Happen **In Planes**

1) A plane of movement is an imaginary <u>flat surface</u> which runs through the body.
2) Planes are used to describe the <u>direction</u> of a movement.
3) When you move a body part (or your whole body), it moves <u>in a plane</u>.
4) There are <u>three</u> planes of movement you need to know:

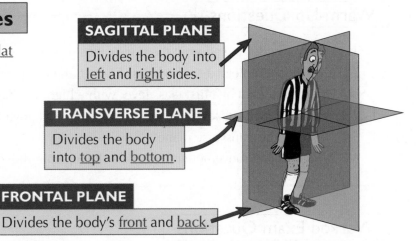

SAGITTAL PLANE
Divides the body into <u>left</u> and <u>right</u> sides.

TRANSVERSE PLANE
Divides the body into <u>top</u> and <u>bottom</u>.

FRONTAL PLANE
Divides the body's <u>front</u> and <u>back</u>.

Movements Happen **Around Axes**

- An axis of movement (two or more are called '<u>axes</u>') is an <u>imaginary line</u> which runs through the body.
- When a body part (or your whole body) moves, it moves <u>around</u> (or '<u>about</u>') an axis.
- There are <u>three</u> types of axis you need to know:

SAGITTAL AXIS
Runs through the body from <u>front to back</u>.

TRANSVERSE AXIS
Runs through the body from <u>left to right</u>.

LONGITUDINAL AXIS
Runs through the body from <u>top to bottom</u>.

Movements use **Different Planes** and **Axes**

Have a look at page 6 for more examples of the movement types.

Every body movement uses <u>both</u> a <u>plane</u> and an <u>axis</u>.
Learn the plane and axis <u>pairs</u> for these <u>movement types</u> and <u>sporting examples</u>.

MOVEMENT TYPE	MOVEMENT DIRECTION	PLANE	AXIS	SPORT MOVEMENTS
flexion/extension	forwards or backwards	sagittal	transverse	tucked and piked somersaults, running, forward roll
abduction/adduction	left or right	frontal	sagittal	cartwheel
rotation	clockwise or anticlockwise	transverse	longitudinal	full twist jump (trampolining), discus throw rotation, ice skating spin

These plane and axis pairs are always <u>the same</u>, e.g. movements that happen in the <u>transverse plane</u> always happen around the <u>longitudinal axis</u>.

There are lots of new terms here to get your head around...

The plane and axis combinations are always the same — make sure you learn the pairs for the exam.
As well as the sports movements in the table, you should think of your own examples too.

Warm-Up and Worked Exam Questions

Movement analysis can be quite a tricky topic — luckily, there are some questions here so you can check it's all sunk in properly.

Warm-Up Questions

1) What provides the effort in the body's lever systems?
2) Give an example of a second class lever in the body.
3) Draw a diagram of a first class lever with a high mechanical advantage.
4) Why do third class levers have a low mechanical advantage?
5) Describe the transverse plane.
6) Which axis of movement does an ice skating spin move around?

Worked Exam Questions

1 Identify the movement plane that divides the body into left and right sides. (Grade 1-3)

The sagittal plane.

[1 mark]

2 **Figure 1** shows a diagram of a lever system. (Grade 3-5)

Weight (resistance) arm △ Effort arm

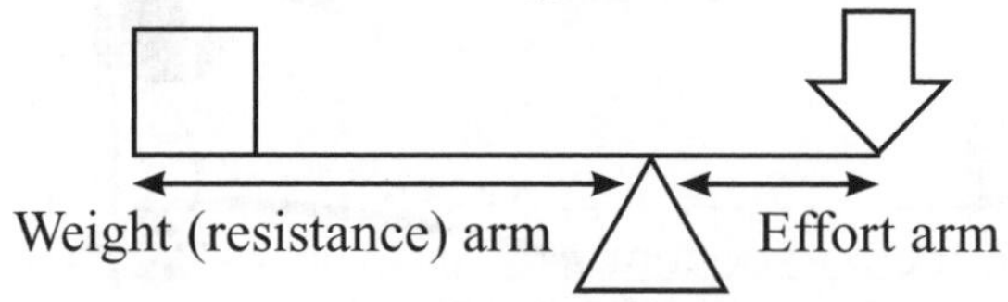

Figure 1

Interpret the mechanical advantage of the lever shown in **Figure 1**.

The lever will have a low mechanical advantage, because the effort arm is shorter

than the weight arm.

[2 marks]

3 When kicking a football, a lever system operates (Grade 5-7) to move the knee joint from flexion to extension.

Identify the load, fulcrum and effort in this lever system.

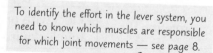
To identify the effort in the lever system, you need to know which muscles are responsible for which joint movements — see page 8.

The load is the weight of the lower leg below the knee, the fulcrum is

the knee joint and the effort is the force of the quadriceps.

[2 marks]

Exam Questions

1   Which **one** of these is the name of the axis that runs through the body from top to bottom? *(Grade 1-3)*

Shade **one** oval only.

A   Sagittal   ⬭

B   Transverse   ⬭

C   Frontal   ⬭

D   Longitudinal ⬭

[1 mark]

2   Identify the plane **and** the axis used during the following movements. *(Grade 3-5)*

(a) Cartwheel

....

....

[2 marks]

(b) Chest pass (in netball)

....

....

[2 marks]

(c) Hammer throw

....

....

[2 marks]

3   A gymnast uses the body's lever systems to stand on their toes.

(a) State the lever class operating at the ankle as the gymnast stands on their toes. *(Grade 3-5)*

....

[1 mark]

(b) Explain how the lever operating at the ankle assists *(Grade 7-9)* the gymnast when standing on their toes.

> Think about the benefits of the lever class you gave in part (a), and how they would help someone to stand on their toes.

....

....

....

....

....

[3 marks]

Revision Summary

Knowledge Organiser   Quick Quiz

That's Movement Analysis all wrapped up. To test yourself before moving on, you can:

- Use the **Knowledge Organiser** to go over all the **key points**.
- Try an **online quiz** for a quick bit of **extra practice** on Sections One and Two.
- Tackle the **summary questions** below. Yes, they're hard — try to answer them **from memory** to **really test** how well you know the topic. The **answers** are all **in the section**, so go over anything **you're unsure of** again.

Lever Systems (p.27-28) ☑

1) Name the four components of a lever system.

2) Which class of lever is shown in the diagrams below?

a)
load
effort   fulcrum

b)

c)

3) Which class of lever is used in dorsiflexion and plantar flexion?

4) Which class of lever is used in elbow flexion? What about elbow extension?

5) a) What is the effort arm of a lever? What is the weight (resistance) arm?
   b) Sketch each class of lever and label these arms on each of them.

6) How do you calculate the mechanical advantage of a lever?

7) What does it mean if a lever system in the body has a:
   a) low mechanical advantage?
   b) high mechanical advantage?

8) Which class of lever always has a:
   a) low mechanical advantage?
   b) high mechanical advantage?

9) When does a first class lever have a high mechanical advantage? When does it have a low mechanical advantage?

Planes and Axes of Movement (p.29) ☑

10) What is a plane of movement? What are they used to describe?

11) Which plane of movement divides:
    a) the top and bottom of the body?
    b) the left and right sides of the body?
    c) the front and back of the body?

12) What is an axis of movement?

13) Which axis runs through the body from:
    a) top to bottom?
    b) front to back?
    c) left to right?

14) Draw a table like this:

Movement type	Movement direction	Plane	Axis	Example of movement in sport
flexion/extension				
abduction/adduction				
rotation				

Now see how much of it you can fill in.

Components of Fitness

First up in section three, two important definitions you'll need: **health** and **fitness**.

Fitness is just **One Part** of being **Healthy**

1) Being healthy is <u>more</u> than just having a healthy body. The <u>World Health Organisation</u> (WHO) say:

> <u>Health</u> is a state of complete <u>physical</u>, <u>mental</u> and <u>social well-being</u>
> and <u>not</u> merely the absence of disease or infirmity.

2) <u>Fitness</u> is one part of <u>good health</u> — here's the definition:

> <u>Fitness</u> is the ability to meet/cope with the <u>demands of the environment</u>.

So, being fit means you're <u>physically able</u> to do whatever you <u>want</u> or <u>need</u> to do, without tiring.

3) Fitness <u>helps</u> with <u>physical</u> health, but you can have a <u>high</u> level of fitness <u>without</u> necessarily being physically healthy — e.g. some athletes <u>overtrain</u> and end up getting <u>injured</u>.

4) <u>Mental</u> and <u>social</u> well-being is also part of being healthy — being unhappy all the time isn't healthy.

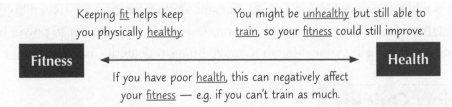

Keeping <u>fit</u> helps keep you physically <u>healthy</u>.

You might be <u>unhealthy</u> but still able to <u>train</u>, so your <u>fitness</u> could still improve.

Fitness ← → Health

If you have poor <u>health</u>, this can negatively affect your <u>fitness</u> — e.g. if you can't train as much.

Cardiovascular Endurance — Getting **Oxygen** to the **Muscles**

- Your <u>heart</u> and <u>lungs</u> work together to keep your muscles <u>supplied with oxygen</u>. The <u>harder</u> you work your muscles, the <u>more oxygen</u> they need.

> <u>CARDIOVASCULAR ENDURANCE</u> is the ability of the <u>heart</u> and <u>lungs</u> to <u>supply oxygen</u> to the working muscles.

- So if you have a <u>high level</u> of cardiovascular endurance (also called <u>aerobic power</u>), your body is able to supply the oxygen your muscles need to do <u>moderately intense</u> whole-body exercise for a <u>long time</u>.
- Most sports require good cardiovascular endurance. For example, a squash player needs to be able to <u>keep</u> up a fast pace <u>all game</u>. If a tennis player finds they are getting <u>tired</u> and losing points <u>late on</u> in a match, they will want to work on their <u>aerobic power</u>.
- A high level of <u>cardiovascular endurance</u> is particularly important for <u>endurance sports</u> like <u>cycling</u>.

Muscular Endurance — How **Long** 'til You get **Tired**

1) When you work your muscles they can get <u>tired</u> and start to feel <u>heavy</u> and <u>weak</u> (<u>fatigued</u>).

> <u>MUSCULAR ENDURANCE</u> is the ability to <u>repeatedly</u> use muscles <u>over a long time</u>, without getting <u>tired</u>.

2) Muscular endurance is really important in any physical activity where you're using the <u>same muscles</u> again and again — e.g. in <u>racquet sports</u> where you have to <u>repeatedly</u> swing your arm.

3) It's also important towards the <u>end</u> of any <u>long-distance race</u> — <u>rowers</u> and <u>cyclists</u> need muscular endurance for a strong <u>sprint finish</u>.

Feeling fit and healthy ready for this section...

Make sure you understand how <u>health</u> and <u>fitness</u> are related to each other before you move on.

Components of Fitness

Three more components of fitness on this page: **strength**, **speed** and **power**. Learn what they are — then make sure you learn what sports and activities each one's important in as well. Right, here we go...

Strength — the Force a Muscle can Exert

1) <u>Strength</u> is just how <u>strong</u> your muscles are.

> **<u>STRENGTH</u> is the amount of <u>force</u> that a muscle or muscle group can apply against a <u>resistance</u>.**

2) It's very important in sports where you need to lift, push or pull things using a lot of <u>force</u>, like <u>weightlifting</u> and <u>judo</u>.

3) Sports that require you to <u>hold</u> your own <u>body weight</u> also need a lot of strength — like the <u>parallel bars</u> and <u>rings</u> in <u>gymnastics</u>.

4) Strength can be broken down into different types:

- <u>Maximal strength</u> is the <u>most</u> amount of force a muscle group can create in a <u>single movement</u>.
- <u>Static strength</u> is when the muscles <u>don't move</u>, but still apply a <u>force</u> — e.g. when <u>holding a handstand</u>.
- <u>Explosive strength</u> uses a muscle's strength in a short, fast <u>burst</u> — it's similar to <u>power</u> (see below).
- <u>Dynamic strength</u> means using your strength to <u>move</u> things <u>repeatedly</u>, like <u>muscular endurance</u> (p.33).

Speed — How Quickly

1) <u>Speed</u> is a measure of how <u>quickly</u> you can do something.

2) This might be a measure of how quickly you <u>cover a distance</u>. It could also be how quickly you can <u>carry out a movement</u>, e.g. how quickly you can throw a punch.

3) To work out speed, you just <u>divide</u> the <u>distance</u> covered by the <u>time</u> taken to do it.

4) Speed is important in lots of activities, from the obvious like a <u>100 m sprint</u>, to the less obvious (like the speed a hockey player can <u>swing their arm</u> to whack a ball across the pitch).

> **<u>SPEED</u> is the <u>rate</u> at which someone is able to <u>move</u>, or to cover a <u>distance</u> in a given amount of <u>time</u>.**

Power Means Speed and Strength Together

> **<u>POWER</u> is a combination of <u>speed</u> and <u>strength</u>.**

> **power = strength × speed**

Most sports need power (also called <u>anaerobic power</u>) for some things. It's important for <u>throwing</u>, <u>hitting</u>, <u>sprinting</u> and <u>jumping</u> — e.g. in the <u>long jump</u>, both the sprint <u>run-up</u> and the <u>take-off</u> from the board require <u>power</u>. Here are some more examples:

SPORT	YOU NEED POWER TO...
Football	...shoot
Golf	...drive
Table tennis	...smash
Tennis	...serve and smash
Cricket	...bowl fast and bat

<u>Coordination</u> and <u>balance</u> (see next page) also help to make the most of power — an <u>uncoordinated</u> or <u>off-balance</u> action will <u>not</u> be as powerful.

EXAM TIP

I have the power...

Make sure you're specific about how components of fitness are used in different activities — e.g. instead of just saying 'strength helps in gymnastics' say 'strength helps the gymnast hold their body weight on the parallel bars'. This shows the examiner you really know your stuff.

Components of Fitness

Now it's time to look at **agility**, **balance** and **coordination** — just like the components of fitness on the last two pages, you need to be able to judge their **importance** for different activities.

Agility — **Control** Over Your Body's Movement

1) Agility is important in any activity where you've got to run about, <u>changing direction</u> all the time, like <u>football</u> or <u>hockey</u>.

2) <u>Jumping</u> and <u>intercepting</u> a pass in <u>netball</u> or <u>basketball</u> involves a high level of <u>agility</u> too.

> <u>AGILITY</u> is the ability to change <u>body position</u> or <u>direction</u> <u>quickly</u> and with <u>control</u>.

Balance — More Than **Not Wobbling**

Having a good sense of <u>balance</u> means you <u>don't wobble</u> or <u>fall over</u> easily. Here's a slightly <u>fancier</u> definition. ➞

> **BALANCE** is the ability to keep the body's <u>centre of mass</u> over a <u>base of support</u>.

1) You can think of the <u>mass</u> of any object as being <u>concentrated</u> at just <u>one point</u>. This point is called the <u>centre of mass</u> (or <u>centre of gravity</u>).

2) <u>Everything</u> has a centre of mass — and that includes <u>us</u>.

3) As you <u>change</u> body position, the <u>location</u> of your centre of mass will change too.

4) Whatever activity you're doing, you need to have your centre of mass <u>over</u> whatever is <u>supporting</u> you (your <u>base of support</u>) to <u>balance</u>. If you don't, you'll <u>fall over</u>.

This is true whether you're <u>moving</u> (<u>dynamic balance</u>)...

...changing <u>orientation</u> and <u>shape</u> (like in dance and gymnastics)...

...or just staying still (<u>static balance</u>).

centre of mass

Base of support: Geoff

Base of support: arms

Base of support: legs

5) Balance is <u>crucial</u> for nearly every physical activity. Any sport that involves <u>changing direction</u> quickly — like <u>football</u> or <u>basketball</u> — requires good <u>balance</u>.

6) An action that is performed with balance is more <u>efficient</u> — e.g. a <u>cyclist</u> might work on improving their balance to <u>increase</u> the speed they can go round <u>corners</u>.

Coordination — Using Body Parts Together

> <u>COORDINATION</u> is the ability to use <u>two or more</u> parts of the body <u>together</u>, <u>efficiently</u> and <u>accurately</u>.

- <u>Hand-eye coordination</u> is important in sports that require <u>precision</u>. E.g. being able to hit a ball in <u>tennis</u>, or shoot a bull's-eye in <u>archery</u>.
- <u>Limb coordination</u> allows you to be able to <u>walk</u>, <u>run</u>, <u>dance</u>, <u>kick</u>, <u>swim</u>...
- Coordinated movements are <u>smooth</u> and <u>efficient</u>. E.g. a <u>runner</u> with well coordinated arms and legs will be able to run <u>faster</u> than someone who is less coordinated.
- Limb coordination is really important in sports like <u>gymnastics</u> or <u>platform diving</u>, where your performance is judged on your coordination.

Agility, Balance and Coordination — as easy as ABC...

<u>Agility</u>, <u>balance</u> and <u>coordination</u> all go together really. You can't be agile if you're not balanced and coordinated. Make sure you learn the definitions of all three and what sporting actions they help with.

Components of Fitness

You're nearly there now, just **two** more components to go — **reaction time** and **flexibility**.

Reaction Time — The Time It Takes You to React

REACTION TIME is the <u>time</u> taken to <u>move in response</u> to a <u>stimulus</u>.

1) In many sports and activities, you need to have <u>fast reactions</u>.

2) The <u>stimulus</u> you respond to could be, e.g. a <u>starter gun</u>, a <u>pass</u> in football, or a <u>serve</u> in tennis.

3) You need fast reactions to be able to <u>hit a ball</u> or <u>dodge a punch</u>.
It doesn't matter how fast you can move, if you don't <u>react in time</u> you'll miss or get hit.

4) Having fast reactions can effectively give you a <u>head start</u>.

Getting away quickly at the start of a <u>sprint</u> can mean the difference between winning and losing.

Having <u>faster</u> reactions in team sports can help you <u>get away</u> from your opponents, so you can get into better playing <u>positions</u>.

Flexibility — Range of Movement

1) <u>Flexibility</u> is to do with <u>how far</u> your joints move. This depends on the <u>type of joint</u> and the 'stretchiness' of the <u>muscles</u> around it.

FLEXIBILITY is the <u>amount of movement</u> possible at a <u>joint</u>.

2) It's often forgotten about, but <u>flexibility</u> is useful for <u>any</u> physical activity. Here's why...

- **FEWER INJURIES**:
  If you're <u>flexible</u>, you're <u>less likely</u> to <u>pull</u> or <u>strain</u> a muscle or stretch too far and injure yourself.

- **BETTER PERFORMANCE**:
  You can't do some activities <u>without</u> being flexible — e.g. doing the <u>splits</u> in <u>gymnastics</u>.

  Flexibility makes you <u>more efficient</u> in other sports so you use less <u>energy</u> — e.g. <u>swimmers</u> with better flexibility can move their arms <u>further</u> around their <u>shoulders</u>. This makes their strokes <u>longer</u> and <u>smoother</u>.

- **BETTER POSTURE**:
  Bad posture can <u>impair breathing</u> and damage your <u>spine</u>.

  More flexibility means a <u>better posture</u> and <u>fewer aches and pains</u>.

Some Components are More Important than Others

1) To be good at <u>any</u> physical activity, you're going to need to have a <u>high level</u> of a <u>number</u> of different <u>components</u> of fitness.

2) For a particular activity, there will always be some components of fitness which are <u>more important</u> than others — e.g. in <u>weightlifting</u>, your <u>strength</u> is more important than your <u>reaction time</u>.

3) To compare the importance of different components, think about the <u>kinds of actions</u> the performer does — e.g. a batsman in <u>cricket</u> has to <u>react</u> to the bowler (<u>reaction time</u>), <u>hit</u> the ball (<u>coordination</u> and <u>power</u>), and then <u>run</u> (<u>speed</u> and <u>cardiovascular endurance</u>).

But all components are important for the exam...

Congratulations, you've made it. No more components of fitness to learn. Now, list all the components of fitness, and give an example of a sport that each one is important for.

Fitness Testing

So, you know what the **components of fitness** are — now you need to know how to **measure** them...

Fitness Testing Helps Identify Strengths and Weaknesses

Fitness testing gives you <u>data</u> that you can <u>analyse</u> to help <u>improve</u> your fitness.

- <u>Fitness tests</u> are designed to <u>measure</u> specific <u>components of fitness</u>. It's important you choose the <u>right</u> one for the <u>specific component</u> you're interested in — otherwise the test is <u>meaningless</u>.
- You can use fitness testing to measure your level of fitness <u>before starting</u> a <u>training programme</u>. The data will show your <u>strengths</u> and <u>weaknesses</u>, so you can plan a personal exercise programme that <u>focuses</u> on what you need to <u>improve</u>.
- The data from fitness tests can be compared with <u>national averages</u> (see p.40).
- You can carry out fitness tests <u>throughout</u> a training programme to <u>provide variety</u> and to <u>monitor</u> your <u>progress</u> to see whether or not the training you're doing is <u>working</u>. This can help to <u>motivate</u> you by showing you where you're <u>improving</u>, and can help you to set yourself <u>new goals</u>.

These Tests are for Muscular Strength...

HANDGRIP DYNAMOMETER TEST — STRENGTH

<u>Equipment</u> needed: a dynamometer.

1) A <u>dynamometer</u> is a device used to measure <u>grip strength</u> — the strength in the <u>hand</u> and <u>forearm</u>.

2) You <u>grip</u> as hard as you can for about <u>five seconds</u> and <u>record</u> your reading in <u>kilograms</u>.

3) Usually, you do this <u>three</u> times and take your <u>best score</u> — the <u>higher</u> the score, the <u>stronger</u> your grip.

ONE REP MAX — MAXIMAL STRENGTH

<u>Equipment</u> needed: gym weight equipment.

1) The aim here is to find the <u>heaviest weight</u> you can <u>lift safely</u> using a particular <u>muscle group</u>. The <u>heavier</u> this weight, the <u>stronger</u> the <u>muscle group</u>.

2) <u>Start</u> with a <u>weight</u> you know you <u>can lift</u>. Once you <u>successfully</u> lift it, <u>rest</u> for a few minutes.

3) <u>Increase</u> the weight you attempt in <u>small steps</u> until you reach a weight with which you <u>can't complete</u> a <u>single lift</u>. The <u>last</u> weight you managed to <u>successfully lift</u> is your <u>one rep max</u>.

This Test is for Muscular Endurance...

SIT-UP BLEEP TEST

<u>Equipment</u> needed: a metronome and a non-slip surface.

- The aim is to stick to a <u>set pace</u> of <u>20 sit-ups a minute</u>.
- The test is <u>finished</u> either when you <u>fail</u> to do a full sit-up in time <u>twice</u> in a row, or if you keep going for <u>four minutes</u>.
- You count <u>how many</u> sit-ups you complete. The <u>more</u> you do the <u>better</u> your <u>abdominal muscular endurance</u>.

You need a good grip of these tests, so sit up and pay attention...

To remember which component of fitness is measured by which test, think about the <u>action</u> you're doing. If you're generating lots of <u>force</u> at once, it's testing <u>strength</u>, but if you're <u>repeating</u> a strength action, it's testing <u>muscular endurance</u>. Repeat it over and over to yourself, and test your own brainular endurance...

Fitness Testing

The first three tests on this page all involve **running**, then there's a **jumping** test for power.

Test your Agility, Speed and Cardiovascular Endurance...

ILLINOIS AGILITY TEST — AGILITY

<u>Equipment</u> needed: stopwatch, cones and a tape measure.

- Set out a <u>course</u> using cones like this.
- Start <u>lying face down</u> at the start cone. When a start whistle blows, run around the course as fast as you can.
- The course is set up so you have to constantly <u>change direction</u>. The <u>shorter the time</u> (in seconds) it takes you to complete the course, the <u>more agile</u> you are.

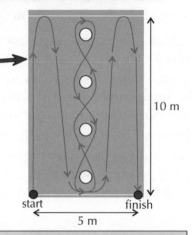

10 m

start   finish

5 m

30 m SPRINT TEST — SPEED

<u>Equipment</u> needed: stopwatch, tape measure and cones.

- Run the 30 m (between cones) <u>as fast as you can</u> and record your time in <u>seconds</u>. The <u>shorter the time</u>, the <u>quicker</u> you are.
- The sprint test can be done over <u>different distances</u>, 50 m is often used.

MULTI-STAGE FITNESS TEST (MSFT) — CARDIOVASCULAR ENDURANCE

<u>Equipment</u> needed: tape measure, cones, multi-stage fitness test recording and some speakers.

1) A recording of a series of <u>timed bleeps</u> is played. You have to run 'shuttles' between two lines (marked by cones), 20 metres apart, starting on the first bleep.

2) Your foot must be <u>on</u> or <u>over</u> the next line when the next bleep sounds.

3) As it gets more difficult, the time between the bleeps gets <u>shorter</u> so you have to <u>run</u> faster.

4) If you miss a bleep, you are allowed two further bleeps to catch up. If you miss <u>three</u> bleeps in total, the <u>level</u> and <u>number</u> of shuttles completed are noted as your final score.

5) The <u>higher</u> the <u>level</u> and <u>number of shuttles</u> completed, the <u>better</u> your <u>cardiovascular endurance</u>.

You can Test your Power by Jumping...

VERTICAL JUMP TEST

<u>Equipment</u> needed: chalk, tape measure and a wall.

1) Put chalk on your fingertips and stand <u>side-on</u> to a wall.

2) Raise the arm that's nearest the wall and mark the <u>highest point</u> you can reach.

3) Still standing side-on to the wall, <u>jump and mark the wall</u> as high up as you can.

4) Measure <u>between</u> the marks in <u>centimetres</u>. The <u>larger</u> the distance, the more <u>powerful</u> your leg muscles are.

I wonder what the Illinois <u>agility</u> test measures...

There's nothing too tricky on this page — just learn which test measures which component of fitness. It's worth thinking about how the tests are better suited for different performers — e.g. the multi-stage fitness test is a more suitable test for a long-distance runner than a sprinter.

Fitness Testing

This page has **four** more tests for you to learn. They're for **flexibility**, **coordination**, **balance** and **reaction time**.

These Tests are for **Flexibility** and **Coordination**...

SIT AND REACH TEST — FLEXIBILITY

Equipment needed: ruler or tape measure and a box.

1) This test measures flexibility in the back and lower hamstrings.

2) You sit on the floor with your legs straight out in front of you and a box flat against your feet.

3) You then reach as far forward as you can and an assistant measures the distance reached in centimetres — the further you can reach, the more flexible your back and hamstrings are.

4) The distance reached can be measured in different ways — usually it's how many centimetres past your toes that you manage to reach.

WALL TOSS TEST — COORDINATION

Equipment needed: stopwatch, a ball and a wall.

1) This tests hand-eye coordination.

2) Start by standing 2 m away from a wall.

3) Throw a ball underarm from your right hand against the wall and catch it in your left hand — then throw it underarm from your left hand against the wall and catch it in your right hand. You repeat this for 30 seconds and count the number of catches.

4) The more successful catches you make, the better your coordination.

5) This is sometimes called the 'alternative hand throw' or 'wall throw' test.

These Tests are for **Balance** and **Reaction Time**...

STORK STAND TEST — BALANCE

Equipment needed: stopwatch.

1) Stand on your best leg with your other foot touching your knee and your hands on your hips.

2) Raise your heel so you're standing on your toes and time how long you can hold the position for in seconds. Wobbling is allowed, but the test finishes if your heel touches the ground, or your other foot or hands move.

3) You usually take the best of three times in seconds — the longer the time, the better your balance.

RULER DROP TEST — REACTION TIME

Equipment needed: ruler.

1) Get a friend to hold a ruler vertically between your thumb and first finger. The 0 cm mark on the ruler should be in line with the top of your thumb.

2) Your friend drops the ruler — you have to try and catch it as soon as you see it drop.

3) Read off the distance the ruler fell before you managed to catch it.

4) The slower your reactions, the longer it takes you to catch the ruler, so the further up the ruler you'll catch it. This means the smaller the distance recorded, the quicker your reaction time.

Here's another test for you...

Using the last two pages, write down the tests for agility, speed, cardiovascular endurance, power, flexibility, coordination, balance and reaction time. Note the equipment needed for each test.

Fitness Testing

You need to understand that these fitness tests are **not perfect**. But they still give you lots of useful **data**.

These **Fitness Tests** have their **Limitations**

When using any of the fitness tests, you need to consider their limitations:

1) Many of the tests do not test specific sporting actions or the movements involved in an activity.

2) Fitness tests may not tell you how an athlete will actually perform under pressure in a competition.

3) Maximal tests require working at maximum effort — e.g. the one rep max test. The results of these tests will not be accurate if the performer is not motivated to work as hard as they possibly can.

4) Many tests do not involve direct measurement and submaximal tests may be used with a formula to predict the maximum performance — so results can be inaccurate.

5) For some of the tests, you might get better scores just by getting more practice at taking the test, without the relevant component of fitness improving.

> Procedures must be followed correctly to make sure the tests are valid and reliable:
> *   If a test is valid, this means it tests the component of fitness that it's supposed to test.
> *   If a test is reliable, it will give the same results if it's repeated under the same conditions. So if you see an improvement in the score, it must be because the athlete is doing better at the test.

All these **Tests** give you **Data** about your **Fitness Levels**

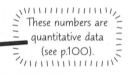

These numbers are quantitative data (see p.100).

Fitness testing gives you a number — e.g. a score, a distance, a time, etc. This is data that you can analyse to assess your fitness levels and make decisions.

1) You can compare your data over time to see how your training is going — e.g. if each week you're recording a bigger distance on the vertical jump test, you know you're increasing your leg power. There's an example of comparing data over time on page 101 — go and have a peek if you like...

2) You can also compare your own performance in a fitness test with average ratings. This can tell you how you rank compared to other people of the same sex in your age group.

3) Each type of fitness test will have a table that you can compare your results with.

> The table below shows average ratings for 16 to 19 year-olds taking the handgrip dynamometer test. Let's say you want to find the rating for an 18-year-old female student who scored 26 kg:

'>' means 'greater than', '<' means 'less than'.

Rating	Excellent	Good	Average	Fair	Poor
Male	> 56 kg	51-56 kg	45-50 kg	39-44 kg	< 39 kg
Female	> 36 kg	31-36 kg	25-30 kg	19-24 kg	< 19 kg

① Choose the row that matches their sex.

② Then read along to find the range of numbers that includes their score.

③ Finally, go up to see which column this range is in — that gives you the rating.

> So, an 18-year-old female student who scored 26 kg on the handgrip dynamometer test has average grip strength for her sex.

I have a new revision workout for you — number crunches...

Analysing data might not be your favourite way to spend time, but it's key to making sense of the results of all the different fitness tests. So, you should really take your time and make sure this stuff has sunk in.

Warm-Up and Worked Exam Questions

Now you've learned everything there is to know about components of fitness and fitness testing, you need to check that it's all sunk in. Luckily, there are three whole pages of questions here for you to do just that...

Warm-Up Questions

1) What is meant by 'fitness'?
2) Define 'muscular endurance'.
3) Which one of the following needs static strength — a gymnast holding a handstand, a sprinter leaving the starting blocks or someone doing a set of press-ups?
4) What is power a combination of?
5) Is agility more important for a 100 m sprinter, or a squash player?
6) Give one example of when a gymnast would need good balance.
7) What is meant by 'reaction time'?
8) How can a high level of flexibility help to prevent injury?
9) Name a test for: a) cardiovascular endurance, b) power, c) coordination
10) Give three limitations of fitness testing.

Worked Exam Questions

1 Define speed **and** identify **one** sporting action where speed is important. (Grade 1-3)

Speed is the rate at which someone can move or cover a distance.

It's needed in hockey to outrun an opponent to the ball.

[2 marks]

There are lots of other examples you could give here for a sporting action that speed helps with — but you only need one to get the mark.

2 Christine trains regularly. She has achieved a high level of fitness with her training programme.

(a) Define health. (Grade 1-3)

Health is a state of complete physical, mental and social well-being.

[1 mark]

(b) Explain why Christine might not be classed as healthy, despite her high level of fitness. (Grade 3-5)

Christine could have a high level of physical fitness, but still be unhappy or suffering from high stress levels. To be classified as healthy, Christine would need to have a good state of mental and social well-being, as well as being physically fit and healthy.

[2 marks]

There are lots of different answers you could have given here. As long as you link your explanation back to the definition of health, you'll get both marks.

Exam Questions

1   Which **one** of these stages of a 100 m sprint event requires a short reaction time?   *(Grade 1-3)*

Shade **one** oval only.

A   During the warm-up   ◯

B   At the start of the race, when the starter pistol is fired   ◯

C   While accelerating away from the starting blocks   ◯

D   During recovery, after the race is finished   ◯

[1 mark]

2   **Table 1** shows ratings for the Handgrip Dynamometer Test   *(Grade 1-3)*
for people aged 16-19 years old.

Rating	Excellent	Good	Average	Fair	Poor
Male	>56 kg	51-56 kg	45-50 kg	39-44 kg	<39 kg
Female	>36 kg	31-36 kg	25-30 kg	19-24 kg	<19 kg

Table 1

Gabrielle is a 17-year old female student.
She took the handgrip dynamometer test and scored 33 kg.

Identify the correct rating for Gabrielle.
Shade **one** oval only.

A   Good   ◯

B   Average   ◯

C   Fair   ◯

D   Poor   ◯

[1 mark]

3   Ben is training to compete in the shot-put and has been working on his strength.   *(Grade 5-7)*

Identify **two** other components of fitness that Ben should
focus on improving in training. Justify each choice.

1 ....

....

2 ....

....

[4 marks]

Exam Questions

4 Eric is planning a training programme.

(a) Describe **two** ways that Eric can use fitness testing to help him plan and carry out his programme. *(Grade 3-5)*

1 ....

....

2 ....

....

[2 marks]

Eric is training to compete in a triathlon.

(b) Explain why the Multi Stage Fitness Test might be more useful to him than the 30 m sprint test. *(Grade 5-7)*

....

....

....

[3 marks]

After six weeks of training, Eric finds that the level he reaches on the Multi Stage Fitness Test has not increased.

(c) State what this tells Eric about the effectiveness of his training programme. *(Grade 3-5)*

....

[1 mark]

5 Using your knowledge of the sit and reach test and the Illinois agility test, evaluate the suitability of these tests for a footballer.

> Think about which component of fitness each of these tests measures.

....

....

....

....

....

....

....

....

[6 marks]

Principles of Training

Training isn't about running for as long as possible, or lifting the heaviest weights you can.
There's much more to it than that — you need to know how training is **matched** to **different people**.

SPORT — The **Four Principles** of Training

To get the most out of your training, you need to follow these <u>four principles</u>:

S

<u>SPECIFICITY</u> — <u>matching</u> training to the <u>activity</u> and <u>components of fitness</u> to be developed.

Make sure you're training using the <u>muscles</u> and <u>actions</u> you want
to <u>improve</u> — e.g. a <u>cyclist</u> would be better off improving their
muscular endurance on an <u>exercise bike</u> than a <u>treadmill</u>.

You should also match the <u>intensity</u> of your training to the activity you're
training for (see p.46) and to the <u>individual needs</u> of the <u>performer</u>.

P

**<u>PROGRESSIVE OVERLOAD</u> — <u>gradually</u> increasing the amount of <u>overload</u>
so that <u>fitness gains</u> occur without <u>injury</u>.**

The only way to get <u>fitter</u> is to work your body <u>harder</u>
than it <u>normally</u> would — this is called <u>overload</u>.

To overload, you can <u>increase</u> the <u>frequency</u>, <u>intensity</u>,
or <u>time spent</u> training (see next page).

O

This needs to be a <u>gradual</u> process to allow your body time to <u>adapt</u>.
If you try to do too <u>much</u> too <u>quickly</u>, you can end up getting <u>injured</u>.

R

**<u>REVERSIBILITY</u> — any fitness <u>improvement</u> or body
<u>adaptation</u> caused by training will <u>gradually</u>
<u>reverse</u> and be lost when you <u>stop</u> training.**

Unfortunately, it takes longer to <u>gain fitness</u> than to <u>lose fitness</u>.

T

<u>TEDIUM</u> — there needs to be <u>variety</u> in your training, otherwise it can become <u>boring</u>.

If you always train in exactly the same way, it'll become <u>boring</u> and you'll
<u>lose motivation</u>. <u>Variation</u> in training helps to keep it <u>fresh</u> and <u>interesting</u>.

SPORT — a handy way to remember these key principles...

The principles of training are tricky, but if you just remember SPORT you'll be fine.
Try it now — without looking at this page, use SPORT to help you write down and give a
definition of each of the four principles of training.

Principles of Training

The best training programmes aren't just thrown together — they have to be **carefully** planned. Part of this planning is leaving enough time for **rest and recovery**, so your body has time to **adapt** to the training.

Training Programmes can be Planned using FITT

Frequency, Intensity and Time are all part of making sure you overload while you're training.

F = FREQUENCY of training — how often you should exercise.

You can overload by increasing how often you exercise, e.g. gradually increasing the number of training sessions. You need to make sure you leave enough time between sessions to recover though (see below).

I = INTENSITY of training — how hard you should exercise.

You can overload by gradually increasing the intensity of your exercise — e.g. lifting heavier weights. How intensely you train depends on the type of fitness you want to improve (see next page) and your level of fitness — someone who hasn't trained for a while should start at a low intensity and gradually increase.

T = TIME spent training — how long you should exercise for.

You can overload by gradually increasing the time you spend on a certain exercise or by increasing the overall time spent exercising — e.g. making training sessions five minutes longer each week.

T = TYPE of training — what exercises and methods of training you should use.

You need to match the type of exercise and method of training to what it is you're training for — e.g. if you want to improve cardiovascular endurance, you need to do exercise that uses lots of muscles, like running or cycling, and you should select an appropriate method of training, e.g. continuous training (see p.49). Varying types of exercise also helps stop training becoming boring and reduces stress on tissues and joints.

All training programmes need to be constantly monitored to make sure that the activities are still producing overload. As you get fitter your programme will need to change to keep improving your fitness.

Your Body Adapts During Rest and Recovery

1) Training makes your body change to cope with the increased exercise. This means you get fitter.
2) These adaptations take place during rest and recovery, so it's vital you allow enough time between training sessions for the body to adapt.
3) It's also important that you allow enough recovery time between workouts to avoid over training. Over training is when you don't rest enough — it can cause injury by not giving your body enough time to recover from the last training session and repair any damage.
4) When you're training, you need to balance your recovery time with the effects of reversibility.
5) If you rest for too long, you'll lose most of the benefits of having done the training in the first place. If you don't rest enough, you could injure yourself through over training.
6) If you get injured, not only have you got to wait for your injury to heal, but thanks to reversibility your fitness will start to decrease while you do. It doesn't seem fair really...

Someone's been really creative with these acronyms...

Want to be fit? Use FITT — Frequency, Intensity, Time and Type. And remember that recovery time is part of training too, because your body needs time to adapt and repair itself if you want to avoid over training.

Training Target Zones

To improve **aerobic** or **anaerobic fitness**, you need to be training at the **right intensity**. To work this out, you have to do some **calculations** based on your **heart rate**. Don't skip a beat and read on to find out more...

Heart Rate — Heartbeats per Minute

1) Your <u>heart rate</u> is the <u>number of times your heart beats per minute (bpm)</u>.

2) When you exercise, your <u>heart rate increases</u> to increase the <u>blood</u> and <u>oxygen supply</u> to your muscles. The <u>harder</u> you work, the more your <u>heart rate</u> will <u>increase</u>.

3) You can find your theoretical <u>maximum heart rate (MHR)</u> by doing: ➔ MHR = 220 − Age

4) And you can <u>use this value</u> to work out <u>how hard</u> you should work to improve your fitness.

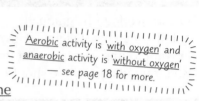

See pages 20-21 for more on how exercise affects your heart rate.

Get your Heart Rate in the Target Zone

- To improve your aerobic or anaerobic <u>fitness</u>, you have to exercise at the <u>right intensity</u>.

- You can do this by making sure that your <u>heart rate</u> is in a <u>target zone</u> — there are different target zones for <u>aerobic</u> and <u>anaerobic training</u>:

  <u>Aerobic</u> activity is '<u>with oxygen</u>' and <u>anaerobic</u> activity is '<u>without oxygen</u>' — see page 18 for more.

  AEROBIC TARGET ZONE — 60%-80% of maximum heart rate.

  ANAEROBIC TARGET ZONE — 80%-90% of maximum heart rate.

- The <u>boundaries</u> of the training zones are called <u>training thresholds</u>. If you're a <u>beginner</u>, you should train nearer the <u>lower</u> threshold. <u>Serious</u> athletes train close to the <u>upper</u> threshold.

Calculating Target Zones — Example

Let's say you want to work out the <u>aerobic target zone</u> for a <u>20-year-old</u>:

1) First, you calculate their <u>maximum heart rate</u> by subtracting their <u>age</u> from 220 — that's <u>220 − 20 = 200</u>.

2) Next you find the <u>thresholds</u>. Because you're calculating the <u>aerobic</u> target zone, the <u>lower</u> threshold is <u>60%</u> of the maximum heart rate — that's <u>200 × 0.6 = 120</u>. The <u>upper</u> threshold is <u>80%</u> of the maximum heart rate — so <u>200 × 0.8 = 160</u>.

3) So the <u>target zone</u> for aerobic training is <u>between 120 and 160 beats per minute</u>.

For the <u>anaerobic</u> thresholds, you'd use 0.8 and 0.9.

Your Training Intensity Should Suit Your Activity

- If you want to be good at an <u>aerobic activity</u>, like <u>long-distance running</u>, then you should do a lot of aerobic activity as part of your training. It improves your <u>cardiovascular system</u>.

- <u>Anaerobic training</u> helps your muscles <u>put up with</u> lactic acid. They also get better at <u>getting rid</u> of it. For <u>anaerobic activity</u> like <u>sprinting</u>, you need to do <u>anaerobic training</u>.

- In many <u>team sports</u>, like lacrosse, you need to be able to move about <u>continuously</u> (aerobic), as well as needing to have <u>spurts</u> of <u>fast movement</u> (anaerobic). You should have a <u>mix</u> of aerobic and anaerobic activities in your training for these.

REVISION TASK

Get in the zone...

Make sure you know the percentages that are used to calculate the thresholds of these target zones. Get some practice by working out your own aerobic and anaerobic target zones...

Warm-Up and Worked Exam Questions

The principles of training can be really tricky, and so can the training target zones. This means you're going to need plenty of practice with this stuff before your exam, which is what the next two pages are for...

Warm-Up Questions

1) What is overload?
2) Give one reason why varying the type of training you do is important.
3) Why is it important to allow time for rest and recovery between exercise sessions?
4) Why does your heart rate change during exercise?
5) Find the maximum heart rate for a 40 year old.
6) What type of activity should a rugby player do in training — aerobic, anaerobic or both?

Worked Exam Questions

1 State **three** methods of achieving overload in training. (Grade 1-3)

1 *You can increase the frequency that you train.*

             You can also achieve overload by varying the type of training you do.

2 *You can increase the intensity of the training.*

3 *You can increase the amount of time each training session lasts.*

[3 marks]

2 In order to improve cardiovascular endurance, training should be done in the aerobic target zone. (Grade 3-5)

Explain how to calculate the thresholds of this training zone.

First calculate 220 — age to find the theoretical maximum heart rate.

The lower threshold of the aerobic training zone is 60% of maximum heart rate.

The upper threshold is 80% of maximum heart rate.

[3 marks]

3 Timothy is a rock climber. He is planning a training programme ahead of an upcoming competition. (Grade 5-7)

Explain why Timothy should think about the principles of reversibility **and** tedium when planning his training programme.

Timothy needs to plan regular training sessions up until the competition to make sure

fitness improvements aren't lost due to reversibility. Timothy needs to use a variety

of training methods, as well as practice climbs, so his training doesn't become boring,

which might cause him to lose motivation.

[2 marks]

Exam Questions

1   Fatima is training for a weightlifting competition. State whether Fatima should spend more of her time training aerobically or anaerobically. Justify your answer.

    (Grade 3-5)

    ....

    ....

    ....

    [2 marks]

2   Lucy is planning a training programme to prepare herself for taking part in a marathon.

    (Grade 3-5)

    (a) Using an example, explain how Lucy could use the principle of progressive overload in her training.

    ....

    ....

    ....

    [2 marks]

    (b) Specificity is another principle of training. Define specificity.

    ....

    ....

    [1 mark]

    (c) Suggest **one** way that Lucy could apply specificity to her training.

    ....

    ....

    ....

    [1 mark]

3   Leonardo is 25 years old. *(Grade 5-7)*

    Calculate the lower threshold of his anaerobic target zone.

    > Remember, to work out target zones, first work out the maximum heart rate.

    ....

    ....

    ....

    [3 marks]

Training Methods

Next up, **training methods**. Remember, you have to match the **type** of training with what you are training for.

Continuous Training Means No Resting

1) Continuous training involves exercising at a steady, constant rate — doing aerobic activities like running or cycling for at least 20 minutes with no breaks. This is also known as steady-state training.

2) It improves cardiovascular endurance and muscular endurance.

3) It usually means exercising so that your heart rate is in your aerobic training zone (see p.46). This means it's good training for aerobic activities like long-distance running.

4) Overload is achieved by increasing the duration, distance, speed or frequency.

ADVANTAGES:
- It's easy to do — going for a run doesn't require specialist equipment.
- Not resting helps prepare for sports where you have to play for long periods of time without a break.

DISADVANTAGES:
- It doesn't improve anaerobic fitness.
- It can become boring doing one exercise at a constant rate.
- It can lead to injury due to repeated use of the same joints / muscles.

Fartlek Training is all about Changes of Speed

1) Fartlek training is a type of continuous training, but it involves changes in the intensity of the exercise over different intervals — e.g. by changing the speed or the terrain (type or steepness of the ground).

> For example, part of a fartlek run could be to sprint for 10 seconds, then jog for 20 seconds (repeated for 4 minutes), followed by running uphill for 2 minutes.

2) It's great for cardiovascular endurance and muscular endurance and also helps to improve speed.

3) You can include a mix of aerobic and anaerobic activity, so it's good training for sports that need different paces, like hockey and rugby.

4) Overload is achieved by increasing the times or speeds of each bit, or the terrain difficulty (e.g. running uphill).

ADVANTAGE:
- It's very adaptable, so you can easily tailor training to suit different sports and different levels of fitness.

DISADVANTAGE:
- Frequent changes to intensity can mean that training lacks structure — this makes it easy to skip the hard bits and tough to monitor progress.

Interval Training uses Fixed Patterns of Exercise

1) Interval training uses fixed patterns of periods of high-intensity exercise and either low-intensity exercise or rest. It has a strict structure. For high-intensity interval training (HIIT) you use maximum effort for the high-intensity bits, and an active, low-intensity rest period.

2) By combining high- and low-intensity work, interval training allows you to improve both cardiovascular endurance and anaerobic fitness. The high-intensity periods can also improve speed.

3) It's great training for sports where you have to move continuously (aerobic), then have sudden spurts of fast movement (anaerobic) — like rugby or water polo.

4) To overload you have to increase the proportion of time spent on the high-intensity exercise, or the intensity — e.g. run faster.

ADVANTAGE:
- It's easily adapted to improve aerobic or anaerobic fitness by changing the intensity and length of work and recovery periods.

DISADVANTAGES:
- Interval training is exhausting. This can make it difficult to carry on pushing yourself.
- Risk of injury due to high intensity.

Training Methods

Weight training helps you to get **stronger**. **Circuit training** lets you do lots of **different** exercises in **one go**.

Weight/Resistance Training works on your Muscles

Weight or resistance training means using your muscles against a resistance. You can use weights, elastic ropes or your own body weight (like in a pull-up or press-up) as the resistance.

Improving your strength will also help increase your power.

1) Weight/resistance training can be used to develop both strength and muscular endurance.

2) It's anaerobic training, so is good for improving performance in anaerobic activities like sprinting.

3) Increasing strength/power means you can hit or kick something harder (hockey, football), throw further (javelin, discus), sprint faster, out-muscle opposition (judo), etc.

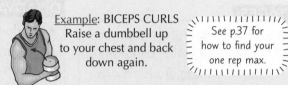

You can train by contracting your muscles to create movement. Each completed movement is called a 'rep' (repetition), and a group of reps is called a 'set'.

Example: BICEPS CURLS Raise a dumbbell up to your chest and back down again.

See p.37 for how to find your one rep max.

- To increase muscular endurance, you use low weight (below 70% of your one rep max) but a high number of reps — approximately three sets of 12-15 reps. To overload, gradually increase the number of reps.

- To increase strength you use high weight (above 70% of your one rep max) but a low number of reps — approximately three sets of 4-8 reps. To overload, gradually increase the weight — but decrease the reps to avoid injury.

- It's important you use the correct lifting technique to prevent injury and lift an appropriate weight to avoid over training.

ADVANTAGES:
- It's easily adapted to suit different sports — you can focus on the relevant muscles.
- Many of the exercises (press-ups, sit-ups, etc.) require little or no equipment.

DISADVANTAGES:
- It puts muscles under high stress levels, so can leave them very sore afterwards.
- If your weightlifting technique is poor, it can be dangerous. Also, some lifts require an assistant.

The assistant is called a 'spotter'.

Circuit Training Uses Loads of Different Exercises

Each circuit has between 6 and 10 'stations' in it. At each station you do a specific exercise for a set amount of time before moving on to the next station.

1) A circuit's stations can work on aerobic or anaerobic fitness — e.g. star jumps for cardiovascular endurance, tricep dips for strength, shuttle runs for speed, etc.

2) You're allowed a short rest between stations. An active rest, e.g. jogging instead of stopping exercising, will improve cardiovascular endurance.

3) Overload is achieved by doing more repetitions at each station, completing the circuit more quickly, resting less between stations, or by repeating the circuit.

ADVANTAGES:
- Because you design the circuit, you can match circuit training to an individual and any component of fitness — e.g. you can improve muscular endurance, strength, cardiovascular endurance... anything you want really.
- Also, the variety keeps the training interesting.

DISADVANTAGE:
- It takes a long time to set up and requires loads of equipment and space.

Learn the pros and cons of these training methods...

Make sure that you understand how weight training can help with muscular endurance and strength. For endurance do low weight, high reps. For strength do high weight, low reps. Say it over and over...

Training Methods

Plyometric training helps make you more **powerful**. **High-altitude training** improves your **cardiovascular endurance** for a **short** amount of time. Pretty intense stuff.

Plyometric Training Improves Power

Loads of sports require explosive strength and power (see p.34), e.g. for fast starts in sprinting, or sports where you need to jump high, like basketball or volleyball. You can train muscular power using plyometrics.

1) When muscles 'contract' to give movement, they either shorten (concentric contraction) or lengthen (eccentric contraction) — see p.8.

2) If a muscle lengthens just before it shortens, it can help to generate power. When a muscle gets stretched and lengthens, extra energy is stored in the muscle (like storing energy in an elastic band by stretching it). This extra energy means the muscle can generate a greater force when it shortens.

3) The extra energy doesn't last very long though. So, the quicker your muscles can move between the lengthening and shortening phases, the more powerful the movement will be.

4) Plyometric training improves the speed you can switch between the two phases, so it improves your power. It's anaerobic exercise and often involves jumping.

Depth jumps are a form of plyometric training. They improve the power of your quadriceps and increase how high you can jump. You drop off a box then quickly jump into the air. The first stage lengthens your quadriceps as you land and squat, the second stage shortens them as you jump.

ADVANTAGE:
- It's the only form of training that directly improves your power.

DISADVANTAGE:
- It's very demanding on the muscles used — you need to be very fit to do it, otherwise you'll get injured.

High-Altitude Training Improves Cardiovascular Endurance

1) At high altitude the air pressure is lower. This means you take in less oxygen with each breath.

2) Your body adapts to this by creating more red blood cells, so enough oxygen can still be supplied to the muscles and organs.

Land at high altitude is a long way above sea level.

3) Some athletes take advantage of this by training at high altitude to increase their red blood cell count. This gives them an advantage when they compete at a lower altitude.

4) More red blood cells means a better oxygen supply to the muscles, so it increases a performer's cardiovascular endurance and muscular endurance. This means it suits endurance athletes.

5) Training at high altitude makes it harder to reach the same intensity levels as you could training at a low altitude, so it's not well suited for anaerobic training.

6) The effects of altitude training only last for a few weeks. Once the athlete returns to a lower altitude, the body doesn't need to create extra red blood cells any more.

ADVANTAGE:
- It improves cardiovascular and muscular endurance, which helps endurance athletes perform better.

DISADVANTAGES:
- The effects only last for a short time.
- It can be very expensive to transport athletes to mountainous regions.
- While at high altitude, you can get altitude sickness. This could mean you lose valuable training time recovering.

Plyometric training — a whole lot of jumping...

In the exam, you might be asked to justify the suitability of a training method for a performer. Think about the actions they use and how the training would help — e.g. 'plyometric training would help a basketball player to jump higher, which would help them to win more rebounds.'

Training Methods

Right, **last** page of training methods. Make sure you understand how the different training methods can be **applied** to **different sports**. Training methods also **differ** in and out of **competition season**...

Static Stretching can be used to Improve **Flexibility**

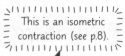
This is an isometric contraction (see p.8).

1) Static stretching is done by gradually stretching a muscle and then holding the position.

2) You hold the stretch at the point where you feel mild discomfort — stretching shouldn't hurt.

3) It's best to do static stretching after a workout, when the muscles are warm.
   To improve flexibility, you should hold the stretches for 30 seconds.

4) To avoid injury you should always stretch gradually. This avoids overstretching the muscle.

5) Static stretching can either be active or passive:

   • In an **ACTIVE** static stretch, you use your own muscles to hold the stretch position.

   • In a **PASSIVE** static stretch, you use someone else or a piece of equipment to help you hold the stretch.

ADVANTAGES:

• It improves flexibility, which can improve athletic performance.

• Almost everyone can do static stretching, even with little previous training.

• It increases the range of movement at a joint.

DISADVANTAGES:

• Poor technique can lead to overstretching and injury.

• It is only effective for stretching certain muscle groups.

Using any of the training methods covered on the last four pages over a period of time has long-term effects on the body's systems. These changes have a positive effect on both your health and performance in physical activity and sport. Make sure you know some examples of sports for which the different training methods are useful.

Training needs to be **Planned Around** when you **Compete**

Most sportspeople don't compete all year round, so they change their training programmes depending on whether it's before, during or after the competition season:

1) **PRE-SEASON (PREPARATION)** — a performer makes sure they're ready for the competitive season. The focus is on general fitness and developing the specific components of fitness and skills they need to compete. E.g. weight training is used to build up strength.

2) **COMPETITION / PLAYING SEASON (PEAK)** — the performer should be at the peak of their fitness and ability. The focus is on maintaining their current level of fitness, and continuing to develop specific skills to improve their performance. If fitness training is stopped, fitness levels will drop (see reversibility, p.44). However, too much training should be avoided so the performer doesn't become fatigued.

3) **POST-SEASON (TRANSITION)** — once the competition season is over, the performer needs to rest and relax to allow their body to recover. Light aerobic training is done to maintain general fitness — e.g. swimming and cycling.

REVISION TASK

Make sure to stretch after this revision workout...

This stuff is really important, and getting it right in the exam could be worth big marks. So, look back over the last four pages and, for each training method, write down two types of performer who would benefit from using it. For each one, add a sentence explaining why.

Preventing Injuries

With any physical activity there's always a **risk** of **injury**. You need to know how to make it as **safe as possible**. After all, injury might **prevent** you from playing sport and, of course, **revising**...

To **Avoid Injury** do These Things...

WARM UP

- See the next page for how to <u>warm up</u> properly...

MAINTAIN HYDRATION

- <u>Drink plenty</u> of water to <u>replace</u> the water lost while <u>exercising</u>. This <u>stops</u> you becoming <u>dehydrated</u> (see p.95).

USE THE CORRECT CLOTHING/EQUIPMENT

- Make sure you're not wearing anything that could get caught (e.g. jewellery, watches).
- Wear suitable <u>footwear</u> — e.g. wearing studded football boots or spiked running shoes can make you less likely to slip and injure yourself.
- Use <u>protective clothing/equipment</u> where appropriate — e.g. gumshields, cycling helmets.

STRUCTURE TRAINING CORRECTLY

- Apply the <u>Principles of Training</u> (see p.44-45).
- This means <u>planning</u> your training <u>correctly</u> — you need to avoid <u>over training</u> and allow enough time for rest and recovery, otherwise you can get <u>overuse injuries</u>. Also, make sure the <u>intensity</u> of exercise matches your level of fitness.

USE TAPING AND BRACING

- You can use special <u>tape</u> or an elastic <u>brace</u> to <u>support joints</u>.
- This restricts the <u>range of movement</u> at a joint, which helps to <u>prevent damage to ligaments</u>.
- It's important that this is done for joints that have been <u>recently injured</u>, to help <u>avoid another injury</u>.

USE THE CORRECT TECHNIQUE

- Make sure that you use the <u>correct technique</u> — e.g. lifting weights properly, stretching without <u>bouncing</u> or <u>overstretching</u>.
- Also, make sure that you use the right technique for <u>moving</u> and <u>carrying</u> equipment.

What you do **After** you **Exercise** is **Important** too...

COOL DOWN

- See next page for how to <u>cool down</u>...

LEAVE ENOUGH RECOVERY TIME

- You need to leave <u>enough time</u> for your body to <u>repair</u> and <u>rebuild</u> after exercise. If you don't you could end up <u>over training</u> (see p.45).

EAT AND REHYDRATE

- Exercising will have <u>used up</u> a lot of the <u>energy</u> stored in your body. You need to <u>replenish</u> this energy, e.g. by eating <u>carbohydrates</u> (see p.94).
- You'll also need to drink plenty of water to <u>rehydrate</u> (see p.95).

ICE BATHS/MASSAGE

- Some athletes will take <u>ice baths</u> or get sports <u>massages</u> following exercise. These may help to prevent <u>delayed onset of muscle soreness (DOMS)</u>.

All this talk of injuries is making my brain hurt...

When you're learning these ways of preventing injury, try to think of how these can be applied to specific activities — for example, think about the different types of equipment needed to play different sports.

Preventing Injuries

Warming up before exercise and **cooling down** afterwards are **vital** — they have tons of benefits. So keep your excitement at a gentle simmer while you **learn** all about them...

Before Exercise you should always Warm Up...

A warm-up gets your body <u>ready</u> for exercise by <u>gradually increasing</u> your work rate. It should involve:

RAISING YOUR PULSE — <u>light exercise</u> increases your <u>heart rate</u> and gets blood flowing to the muscles.

- This raises your body <u>temperature</u> and <u>warms</u> up <u>muscles</u>, <u>ligaments</u> and <u>tendons</u> so they can move more <u>freely</u> and are less likely to get <u>injured</u>. Warmer muscles can also <u>contract</u> more <u>quickly</u>.
- It also helps to <u>ease</u> your body into exercising by <u>gradually</u> increasing the exercise <u>intensity</u>, and it increases the <u>oxygen supply</u> to the <u>muscles</u>.

STRETCHING AND MOBILITY EXERCISES — this increases <u>flexibility</u> at your joints.

- It should <u>focus</u> on the <u>muscles</u> and <u>movements</u> you will <u>use</u> in the activity — e.g. shoulder circles before playing tennis.
- This helps increase the <u>range of movement</u> of your <u>muscles</u> and <u>joints</u>, which will help you <u>perform better</u> and <u>avoid injury</u>.

PRACTICE ACTIONS — e.g. practice shots in netball, throwing and catching in rounders, etc.

- This prepares the <u>muscles</u> that will be <u>used</u> in the activity, so they perform better.
- It also helps with your <u>mental preparation</u>, as it <u>focuses you</u> on the activity and gets you "<u>in the zone</u>".
  You could also use <u>mental preparation techniques</u> so you're calm, confident and focused (see p.65).

...And Afterwards you should Cool Down

A cool-down gets your body <u>back to normal</u> after exercise by <u>gradually decreasing</u> the <u>intensity</u> of work to control your return to resting levels. It should involve:

GRADUALLY REDUCING INTENSITY

— <u>gentle exercise</u> like jogging to keep the <u>heart</u> and <u>lungs</u> working harder than normal. You should <u>gradually reduce</u> the <u>intensity</u> of this exercise so that your <u>heart rate</u>, <u>breathing rate</u> and <u>body temperature</u> decrease gradually.

- This means you can continue taking in more <u>oxygen</u> to help get rid of the <u>lactic acid</u> and other waste products in your <u>muscles</u> (repaying the oxygen debt — see p.19). It also helps you to remove the extra <u>carbon dioxide</u> in your <u>blood</u>.
- It keeps the <u>blood</u> flowing back from the muscles, so stops <u>blood pooling</u> in the legs and arms — blood pooling can cause <u>dizziness</u> and even <u>fainting</u>.

STRETCHING the muscles that have been used to <u>speed up recovery</u> and <u>improve flexibility</u>.

- <u>Static stretching</u> (see p.52) while the muscles are warm helps to improve <u>flexibility</u>.
- It may also help to prevent <u>delayed onset of muscle soreness</u> (DOMS).

Ease into and out of exercise gradually...

Warming up is especially important for more intense, anaerobic activities, where it's easy to get an injury. And don't forget the cool-down — it helps the body to remove lactic acid from the muscles and repay the oxygen debt built up during anaerobic activity. This helps to speed up your recovery.

Warm-Up and Worked Exam Questions

Coming up — three pages of questions about training methods and preventing injuries. Look over the aptly named warm-up and worked exam questions before you try the exam questions for yourself.

Warm-Up Questions

1) What is fartlek training?
2) Describe the difference between a 'rep' and a 'set' in weight training.
3) Name two anaerobic training methods.
4) Give one disadvantage of circuit training.
5) What type of performer would benefit from high-altitude training? Why?
6) Competition season is one of the training seasons for competitive athletes. Name the other two.
7) Why is it important to structure your training?
8) Give an example of something that can be done after a training session to help prevent injury.
9) Why might a performer include practice actions in their warm-up?
10) What should a cool down involve?

Worked Exam Questions

1 Sharon wants to improve her muscular endurance using fartlek training. Grade 1-3

   (a) Identify **one** advantage of fartlek training.

   It is easily adapted to suit an individual's training needs.

   Make sure you know the advantages and disadvantages of all the training methods.

   [1 mark]

   (b) State **two** other types of training that could improve her muscular endurance.

   1 *Continuous training*

   2 *Weight training*

   You could also put circuit training or high-altitude training here.

   [2 marks]

2 Complete **Table 1** to identify **one** training method that improves strength, **one** component of fitness improved by continuous training and **one** long-term effect on the body each method can cause. Grade 3-5

Training method	Component of fitness improved	Long-term effect on the body
Weight	Strength	*Muscular hypertrophy*
Continuous	*Cardiovascular endurance*	*Lower resting heart rate*

Table 1

This final column draws on knowledge from page 22.

[4 marks]

Exam Questions

1 Weight training is a type of training method. (Grade 3-5)

Explain how weight training can be used to improve muscular endurance.

....

....

....

....

[2 marks]

2 N'Golo wants to improve his cardiovascular endurance and his leg strength.

He decides to use circuit training.

(a) State **one** advantage of circuit training. (Grade 1-3)

....

....

[1 mark]

(b) State **one** circuit station N'Golo could use to improve his cardiovascular endurance. (Grade 3-5)

....

[1 mark]

(c) N'Golo includes squats in his circuit, to improve his leg strength.
Suggest **one** way he could adapt his work at this station to increase overload. (Grade 5-7)

....

[1 mark]

3 Mrs Costanza is a PE teacher. She has started an after school hockey club. She always (Grade 5-7) makes sure that students warm up before playing, and cool down afterwards.

Explain what other actions she can take to reduce the risk
of injury to students during hockey club.

....

....

....

....

....

....

[3 marks]

Exam Questions

4 Discuss the appropriateness of static stretching as a training method for an endurance athlete.
Grade 7-9

For this question, make sure you consider both the benefits and the limitations of static stretching for an endurance athlete.

....

....

....

....

....

....

....

[4 marks]

5 Outline what interval and continuous training are, and justify why they are suitable for a basketball player.

....

....

....

....

....

....

....

....

....

....

....

....

....

....

....

[9 marks]

Revision Summary

Knowledge
Organiser

Quick
Quiz

Physical Training isn't over just yet. To keep those revision muscles pumping, why not:

- Use the **Knowledge Organiser** to go over all the **key points**.
- Try an **online quiz** for a quick bit of **extra practice**.
- Tackle the **summary questions** below. Yes, they're hard — try to answer them **from memory** to **really test** how well you know the topic. The **answers** are all **in the section**, so go over anything **you're unsure of** again.

Components of Fitness (p.33-36) ☑

1) What is the full definition of health?
2) How would you explain what fitness is?
3) How can your health affect your fitness? How can your fitness affect your health?
4) What is cardiovascular endurance? How is muscular endurance different?
5) What is... a) strength? b) speed? c) power?
6) How would you explain the difference between agility and flexibility?
7) How might having good balance help your coordination?
8) Give an example of when you would need a fast reaction time in: a) a team sport, b) an individual sport.

Fitness Testing (p.37-40) ☑

9) Why do people do fitness tests?
10) How would you carry out these tests: a) one rep max? b) wall toss? c) stork stand? d) ruler drop? Which component of fitness do they each measure?
11) How would you do a fitness test that measures: a) muscular endurance? b) agility? c) speed? d) power?
12) Describe the multi-stage fitness test. Which component of fitness does it measure?
13) Which component of fitness does the sit and reach test measure? What units are the results usually in?
14) See if you can come up with five different limitations of fitness tests.
15) What is meant by a reliable fitness test? How about a valid test?

Principles of Training & Training Target Zones (p.44-46) ☑

16) What does SPORT stand for (in terms of the principles of training)? What do each of the terms mean?
17) What are the four principles of FITT? How do they each make sure you overload while training?
18) What might happen if you don't rest after training? What about if you rest too much?
19) Describe how to calculate your: a) maximum heart rate, b) aerobic target zone, c) anaerobic target zone.

Training Methods (p.49-52) ☑

20) Copy the table and fill it in for the following training methods: continuous, Fartlek, interval, weight/resistance, circuit training, plyometric, high-altitude and static stretching.

Training method	Description	Advantages	Disadvantages
Continuous			
Fartlek			

21) How are pre-season and playing (competition) season training programmes usually different? How might your post-season (transition) training be different again?

Preventing Injuries (p.53-54) ☑

22) a) List six things you can do while training to avoid getting injured.
   b) What about four things you could do after exercising?
23) What are the key parts of a warm-up? Bonus points for explaining why you need to do each part.
24) a) Why is gentle exercise an important part of a cool-down? b) How about stretching?

Learning Skills

This page is all about the different types of **skill** — so buckle up for plenty of thrilling definitions.

A **Skill** is Something You **Learn**

1) Skill is a word we use all the time. Here's what it means in PE:

> **A SKILL is a <u>learned action</u> to bring about the <u>result</u>**
> **you want with <u>certainty</u> and <u>minimum effort</u>.**

2) So a skill is something you've <u>got to learn</u>. You can't be born with a skill, although you might learn it more easily than other people. How easily you learn a skill is based on your <u>ability</u>:

> **ABILITY is a person's set of <u>traits</u> that control their <u>potential to learn</u> a skill.**

3) In netball, shooting is a <u>skill</u> because it's a <u>learned action</u> to help a player score goals. There are lots of <u>inherited traits</u> that determine a player's <u>ability</u> to become successful at shooting — e.g. <u>composure</u> to stay calm under pressure or <u>balance</u> to keep stable.

There are **Different Types** of **Skill**

1) There are four different <u>skill classifications</u> that you need to know about:

BASIC (SIMPLE) VS COMPLEX SKILLS

- A <u>basic skill</u> is quick to learn as it <u>doesn't</u> need much <u>thought</u> or <u>decision-making</u> e.g. running.
- A <u>complex skill</u> needs <u>lots of decision-making</u> so requires a lot of <u>thought and coordination</u>, e.g. an overhead kick in football.

OPEN VS CLOSED SKILLS

- An <u>open skill</u> is performed in a <u>changing environment</u>, where a performer has to <u>react</u> and <u>adapt</u> to <u>external factors</u>. E.g. during a <u>football tackle</u>, you need to adapt to things such as the position of other players on the pitch.
- A <u>closed skill</u> is always performed in the same <u>predictable environment</u> — it's <u>not</u> affected by external factors. Often the skill involves the <u>same action</u> each time — e.g. when <u>breaking off</u> in snooker, the conditions and movement are always the <u>same</u>.

SELF- VS EXTERNALLY-PACED SKILLS

- A <u>self-paced skill</u> is controlled by the <u>performer</u> — they decide when and how quickly it's done.
- An <u>externally-paced skill</u> is affected by <u>external factors</u>, which control when it starts and how quickly it's done. E.g. an <u>opponent's actions</u> in football might determine when a pass is played and the speed it's played at.

GROSS VS FINE SKILLS

- A <u>gross skill</u> involves <u>powerful</u> movements performed by <u>large muscle groups</u>, e.g. the long jump.
- A <u>fine skill</u> uses <u>smaller</u> muscle groups to carry out <u>precise</u> movements that require <u>accuracy</u> and <u>coordination</u>, e.g. throwing a dart.

2) Many skills come somewhere <u>in between</u> these classifications. You can show this by putting skills on a '<u>continuum</u>' (or '<u>scale</u>') with one category on each end.

3) For example, you can compare the "openness" of skills by putting them on a <u>scale</u> like this one:

4) You can also put sport skills on a scale using the other skill classifications, e.g. a scale from basic to complex skills.

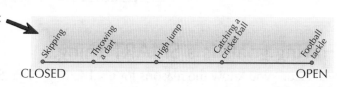

CLOSED   Skipping   Throwing a dart   High jump   Catching a cricket ball   Football tackle   OPEN

Goal Setting

Setting **goals** and **targets** can often seem a bit of a hassle. But if you put the effort in and set them properly, not only do you have something to **aim** for, but reaching your targets can make you feel **ace**.

Goal Setting can Help you Train

- Goal setting means setting targets that you want to reach so you can improve your performance.
- Goal setting helps training by giving you something to aim for, which motivates you to work hard. Also, reaching a goal can boost your confidence and help your emotional well-being (see p.90).
- You can set yourself a performance goal, an outcome goal, or a combination of both:

  PERFORMANCE GOALS — these are based on improving your own personal performance.
  OUTCOME GOALS — these are focused on the end result only, i.e. winning.

- Most of the time, it's better to set performance goals — especially if you're a beginner. Winning might be an unrealistic goal if you're new to a sport, and it can be demotivating if you lose.
- Also, you can't usually control the result of an outcome goal, as it will depend on how well other people perform.

  You need to be able to suggest suitable goals for performers of different sports and abilities.

Goal Setting Should be SMART

When you're setting targets make sure they're **SMART**.

S → **SPECIFIC**: Say exactly what you want to achieve.
  1) You need to have a specific target and outline exactly what you need to do to achieve it.
  2) This makes sure you're focused on your goal.
  3) E.g. 'My goal is to swim 1000 m continuously'.

  Goals should target specific sporting skills, movements or muscles used by the performer.

M → **MEASURABLE**: Goals need to be measurable.
  1) This is so you can see how much you've progressed towards your goal over time — so you stay motivated to train.
  2) E.g. 'My goal is to run 100 m in under 12 seconds'.

A → **ACCEPTED**: Goals should be decided by everyone involved — e.g. a performer and coach. The other people involved can make sure the target is set at the right level of difficulty and can motivate the performer to stay focused on it.

R → **REALISTIC**: Set targets you can realistically reach.
  1) This means making sure you have everything you need to be able to fulfil your target.
  2) That could mean being physically able to do something, or having enough resources (time, money, facilities...) to be able to reach your target.
  3) This is so you stay determined during training — if it's not realistic, you could be put off.

T → **TIME-BOUND**: Set a deadline for reaching your goal.
  1) You need a time limit to make sure your target is measurable.
  2) Meeting short-term target deadlines keeps you on course to reach your long-term goals in time.
  3) This keeps you motivated — you'll want to train to achieve your goal in time for your deadline.

As well as setting targets, you need to make sure you review them regularly. This is so you can see how much you've progressed towards your goal and what else you need to do to achieve it.

Having goals is a SMART thing...

Make sure you know the reasons for goal setting, what SMART stands for and how it improves performance.

Warm-Up and Worked Exam Questions

That's the first few pages of this section done, so it's question time. The warm-up questions and worked exam questions will help get you into exam mode before you do the questions on the next page yourself.

Warm-Up Questions

1) What is a performer's 'ability'?
2) What is a complex skill?
3) Give an example of a closed skill.
4) What is a 'performance goal'?
5) Give one reason why a performer might want to avoid setting an outcome goal.
6) What does the 'M' stand for in a 'SMART' target?
7) Why is it important for a target to be accepted?

Worked Exam Questions

1   'SMART' stands for the five principles of goal setting. **Grade 1-3**

Describe the principle that 'S' represents.

The 'S' in 'SMART' stands for specific, which means a goal should say exactly what the performer wants to achieve.

[1 mark]

2   Skills can be classified as either self-paced or externally-paced. **Grade 3-5**

Define a self-paced skill and an externally-paced skill, and suggest **one** example of each type of skill from sports of your choice.

1 A self-paced skill is controlled by the performer. For example, an athlete decides when to throw a javelin and has total control over their movements.

2 An externally-paced skill is affected by external factors. For example, the position and direction of the ball in cricket determines how a wicket-keeper catches it.

[4 marks]

Don't forget to include the examples
— they're worth half the marks.

3   Discuss whether performing the high jump can be classified as a closed skill. **Grade 7-9**

The high jump can be a closed skill, as it's usually performed in the same environment and uses the same action/technique each time (the 'Fosbury Flop'). However, it's not a completely closed skill, as the run up to the jump can be affected by external factors such as the weather.

[3 marks]

Exam Questions

1   'Measurable' is one of the principles of goal setting.

(a) Explain how this principle can be used to improve sports performance. (Grade 3-5)

....

....

....

[2 marks]

Layla sets herself a goal to run 5 km in 27 minutes.

(b) Identify how this goal applies the 'measurable' principle of goal setting. (Grade 3-5)

....

....

[1 mark]

(c) Explain how Layla could apply **two** other principles of goal setting to make her goal more effective. (Grade 5-7)

....

....

....

....

[4 marks]

2   Classify the skill of performing a somersault using the classifications below: (Grade 5-7)

- basic/complex
- open/closed
- self-paced/externally-paced
- gross/fine

Explain each of your choices.

....

....

....

....

....

....

[4 marks]

Guidance and Feedback

To learn or improve a skill, you might need some **guidance** and **feedback** to help you.

Guidance — How to Perform or Develop a Skill

Have a look at p.59 for definitions of the different skill types.

There are lots of different types of guidance a coach or trainer can give:

VERBAL — An explanation in words of how to perform a technique.

ADVANTAGES	DISADVANTAGES
• Can be combined with other types of guidance. • Helpful for elite performers who'll understand any technical language. • Can give guidance during a performance. This is especially useful for improving open skills.	• Less useful for teaching complex skills, which are difficult to explain. • Could be confusing for a beginner if it uses complicated language.

VISUAL — Visual clues to help you perform a technique. A coach could use demonstrations or videos and diagrams of a technique to show how it should be performed.

ADVANTAGES	DISADVANTAGES
• Works well for beginners — they can copy the skill. • Can be used to teach closed skills — these often repeat the same action each time. • Slow motion videos can be useful to highlight small details of a skill for elite performers.	• Less useful for teaching complex and open skills — they're more difficult to copy. • Demonstrations for beginners must be clear, concise and simple in order to be useful.

MANUAL — When the coach physically moves your body through the technique. For example, a coach might guide your arms when you're practising a golf swing.

ADVANTAGES	DISADVANTAGES
• Useful for teaching beginners — they can get the "feel" of a skill before doing it on their own. • Helpful for teaching complex skills.	• A performer could start to rely on it and not be able to perform a skill without it. • Difficult to use with big groups of learners.

MECHANICAL — Guidance given using sport equipment, e.g. a harness in trampolining.

ADVANTAGES	DISADVANTAGES
• Useful for teaching beginners — they can feel safe while practising a new skill that might normally be dangerous, e.g. a somersault. • Helpful for teaching complex skills.	• A learner might be unable to perform the skill without the help of the equipment. • Difficult to use in large groups.

Feedback — Finding Out How You Did

1) Feedback can be either intrinsic or extrinsic:

INTRINSIC — you know how well you did the technique because of what it 'felt' like. This is called kinaesthetic feedback and works best for elite performers — they can judge how well they've performed.
EXTRINSIC — someone else tells you or shows you what happened, and how to improve. This is suited to beginners — they don't have the experience or knowledge to accurately assess their own performance.

2) You can use feedback to work out your strengths and weaknesses and come up with an action plan to improve your performance.

Using Feedback

More about **feedback** on this page, and how it's **applied** when you **perform** or **practise** a skill.

Feedback can Focus on Different Aspects of a Skill

- The information in feedback can focus on different parts of a skill or movement. It might focus on:

  > **KNOWLEDGE OF PERFORMANCE** — did you use the correct movements/technique? This can be extrinsic or intrinsic. This type of feedback works well for elite performers — it helps them to 'fine-tune' a skill that they can already perform.
  >
  > **KNOWLEDGE OF RESULTS** — what was the outcome? This is usually extrinsic and can include data, e.g. your time in a race. This is useful for beginners — they need to be told whether or not they achieved the right result.

- Feedback could also focus on what you did well (positive feedback), or what you didn't do well and could improve (negative feedback).

- It's better to avoid too much negative feedback with beginners — it can put them off learning the skill. Positive feedback is better — it helps them remember which parts of the movement they should repeat.

- Negative feedback can be useful for elite performers. It can help to motivate them by setting a goal for them to aim for.

Feedback is part of the Information Processing Model

The information processing model divides the process of performing or practising skills into four stages:

1) **INPUT** — when you receive information from the environment through your senses, e.g. seeing and hearing what is happening during a game. This stage involves selective attention (see next page).

2) **DECISION MAKING** — when you decide how to respond to the input. To decide on the best response, you compare what is happening at the time (stored in your short-term memory) with your past experiences of performing the skill (stored in your long-term memory).

4) **FEEDBACK** — after the output, you receive extrinsic or intrinsic feedback (or both). This helps you to improve the skill next time you perform it.

3) **OUTPUT** — Your muscles react to messages from the brain telling them what to do to perform the skill.

You might be asked to draw this model (in boxes) and/or explain the four stages.

You can apply this model to analyse a sports skill. For example, when taking a penalty in football:

1) **INPUT** — You'd need to pay attention to the position of the goalkeeper in front of the net and ignore distractions like noise from the crowd.

2) **DECISION MAKING** — You'd decide on the best way to perform the penalty by using what you've done in your previous practice of penalties.

3) **OUTPUT** — Your brain would send information to your muscles to tell them where to aim the shot and how powerfully to kick the ball.

4) **FEEDBACK** — You'd receive extrinsic feedback, e.g. whether or not you scored the penalty, or your coach telling you what you did right or wrong. You might also get intrinsic feedback. You could learn from this feedback how you could perform a penalty better next time.

Keep going — you're doing really well...

Double-check that you know which types of feedback work best for beginners and elite performers.

Mental Preparation

Who'd have thought it — **performing well** in sport is about **the mind** as well as the body...

You can **Mentally Prepare** for Sport

- Being <u>mentally prepared</u> is all about being able to get in the 'zone'.
- It can help you stay <u>focused</u>, <u>confident</u> and <u>motivated</u>, keep control of your emotions and <u>cope with stress</u> so you can perform at your best.
- There are lots of different techniques to help you <u>mentally prepare</u>:

Techniques 1-5 are also called 'stress management techniques' — they help lower your <u>arousal level</u> (see below).

1) **MENTAL REHEARSAL** is <u>imagining</u> yourself carrying out a <u>movement</u> or <u>skill perfectly</u> or where you picture a <u>positive outcome</u>, e.g. winning a race.

2) **VISUALISATION** involves <u>imagining</u> yourself in a <u>relaxing place</u> to help you feel <u>calm</u>.

3) **DEEP BREATHING** can help <u>lower</u> your <u>heart rate</u> (which <u>increases</u> when you're <u>anxious</u>) and make you feel more <u>calm</u>.

4) **IMAGERY** is used when you <u>imagine</u> being somewhere or doing something — <u>mental rehearsal</u> and <u>visualisation</u> are both types of imagery.

5) **POSITIVE SELF-TALK/ THINKING** is telling yourself <u>positive things</u> that will <u>motivate</u> you or <u>reassure</u> you that you can <u>perform well</u>.

6) **SELECTIVE ATTENTION** is focusing on important things that will help you perform well, and <u>ignoring</u> things that <u>aren't important</u>.

- Practising your skills during a <u>warm-up</u> (see page 54) can also help you mentally prepare.

Your **Arousal Level** shouldn't be **Too High** or **Too Low**

1) Your <u>arousal level</u> is how <u>mentally</u> (and <u>physically</u>) <u>alert</u> you are.
2) To <u>perform well</u> you need to have the right arousal level. The <u>relationship</u> between <u>performance</u> and <u>arousal</u> can be shown on an '<u>inverted-U graph</u>'.
3) The graph shows the '<u>inverted-U theory</u>', which says that:

You might be asked to draw or describe this graph in the exam.

- If your arousal level is <u>low</u>, then you're not very excited and you're <u>unlikely</u> to perform well.
- At <u>higher</u> arousal levels, you'll be <u>determined</u> and <u>ready</u>, and should be able to perform your skills <u>well</u>.
- If your arousal level <u>rises too much</u>, you become <u>anxious</u> and <u>nervous</u>. You might become <u>tense</u>, which can cause you to '<u>choke</u>', so your performance will <u>suffer</u>. You might also become <u>overaggressive</u>.

4) The <u>ideal</u> arousal level <u>varies</u> for different skills in sport.
5) <u>Gross skills</u> require <u>higher arousal</u> levels. E.g. when tackling in <u>football</u>, a <u>higher arousal</u> level will help you commit to putting all of your <u>effort</u> into getting the ball. But if your arousal level is <u>too high</u>, you might end up <u>hurting</u> another player when you tackle them.

The <u>lowest</u> arousal level can be called <u>deep sleep</u> and the <u>highest</u> called <u>intense excitement</u>.

6) When performing a <u>fine skill</u>, you need a <u>lower arousal</u> level. E.g. when <u>fielding</u> in cricket, a <u>lower arousal</u> level will help you keep your hands <u>steady</u> to catch the ball. But your arousal level shouldn't be <u>too low</u> — or you won't be <u>alert enough</u> to move into a good position to catch the ball.

Mentally rehearse your exam for guaranteed success...

Being mentally prepared can really help your performance — so it's lucky that there are some handy techniques to help you on your way to being mentally ready for sport. Make sure you learn them all.

Emotion and Personality

This is the last page to learn in this section — it'll cover the types of **motivation**, **aggression** and **personality**.

Motivation makes you Want to Do Well

1) <u>Motivation</u>'s about how <u>keen</u> you are to do something. It's what <u>drives you on</u> when things get difficult — your <u>desire</u> to succeed.

2) Motivation can be either <u>intrinsic</u> (from yourself) or <u>extrinsic</u> (from outside).

INTRINSIC MOTIVATION
Motivation from the <u>enjoyment</u> and good <u>feelings</u> you get from taking part in physical activity and sport, e.g. pride, high self-esteem.

EXTRINSIC MOTIVATION
Motivation through <u>rewards</u> from other people/ sources. This can be <u>tangible</u> (you can <u>touch it</u>, e.g. trophies, money) or <u>intangible</u> (you <u>can't touch it</u>, e.g. applause, praise from a coach).

3) <u>Intrinsic motivation</u> is usually seen as the <u>most effective</u> — you're more likely to <u>try hard</u> in sport and <u>carry on</u> playing it in the long run if you <u>enjoy it</u>.

4) <u>Extrinsic motivation</u> can also be really <u>effective</u>. Rewards or praise about your performance can make you feel <u>good</u> about yourself — so you're more likely to <u>want</u> to perform well again.

5) But if you <u>don't like</u> a sport, <u>extrinsic</u> rewards on their own probably <u>won't motivate</u> you to <u>try</u> very hard at it, or play it <u>regularly</u>. They work better when you're already <u>intrinsically</u> motivated.

6) But some people think that too many <u>extrinsic</u> rewards can actually <u>reduce</u> your <u>intrinsic</u> motivation — so you might start to <u>rely</u> on extrinsic rewards to feel <u>motivated</u>.

Aggression can be Direct or Indirect

<u>Aggression</u> doesn't have to be <u>violent</u> — when it's used <u>properly</u>, it can improve your <u>performance</u> in sport.

1) <u>Direct aggression</u> involves <u>physical contact</u> with another person, e.g. pushing against the opposing team in a <u>rugby scrum</u> so you can win the ball.

2) <u>Indirect aggression</u> doesn't involve physical contact — a player gains an advantage by aiming the aggression at an <u>object</u> instead. E.g. a golfer performing a drive would use indirect aggression towards the golf ball to hit it powerfully to the green.

Introverts and Extroverts like Different Sports

The <u>type of sport</u> you like can be affected by your <u>personality</u>. You can describe someone as an <u>introvert</u> or an <u>extrovert</u> based on what their personality is like — most people are somewhere <u>in between</u>.

<u>INTROVERTS</u> are <u>shy</u>, <u>quiet</u> and <u>thoughtful</u> — they like being <u>alone</u>.
- Introverts usually prefer sports that they can do <u>on their own</u>.
- They tend to like sports where they'll need <u>fine skills</u>, <u>high concentration</u> and <u>low arousal</u>.
- For example, <u>archery</u>, <u>snooker</u> and <u>athletics</u> are all suited to introverts.

<u>EXTROVERTS</u> are more <u>sociable</u> — they're <u>talkative</u> and prefer being with <u>other people</u>.
- Extroverts might get <u>bored</u> when they're alone, so they usually prefer <u>team sports</u>.
- They also tend to like <u>fast-paced</u> sports that need <u>gross skills</u> and <u>low concentration</u>.
- For example, <u>hockey</u>, <u>rugby</u> and <u>football</u> are well-suited to extroverts.

I hope you're feeling motivated for your PE exams...
There's a handy way to remember what 'intrinsic' and 'extrinsic' mean. '<u>In</u>trinsic' starts with '<u>in</u>', so it comes from <u>inside</u> you. '<u>Ex</u>trinsic' starts with '<u>ex</u>', just like '<u>exit</u>', so it comes from outside.

Warm-Up and Worked Exam Questions

Section Four is nearly done — so check you've taken in the last few pages by doing some questions. Make sure you understand the answers below before you try the exam questions on the next two pages.

Warm-Up Questions

1) Give one advantage of verbal guidance.
2) Where does extrinsic feedback come from?
3) Why is feedback involving knowledge of results useful for beginners?
4) Describe the 'output' stage of the information processing model.
5) What is meant by 'arousal level'?
6) Give one example of direct aggression in sport.
7) Who is more likely to play rugby — an extrovert or an introvert?

Worked Exam Questions

1 Define the term mechanical guidance. (Grade 1-3)

Mechanical guidance is when a performer is given help with ....
performing a skill through the use of sports equipment. ....

[1 mark]

2 Explain the difference between intrinsic and extrinsic motivation. (Grade 1-3)

Intrinsic motivation comes from a performer's positive feelings they get from ....
doing something, whereas extrinsic motivation comes from an outside source. ....

[2 marks]

3 Explain why extrinsic feedback is important to a beginner. (Grade 3-5)

Extrinsic feedback comes from a coach or other person, which is useful for a ....
beginner as they aren't knowledgeable enough to give themselves feedback, ...
so they need someone else to tell them what they are doing right or wrong. ....

[3 marks]

4 Describe, using **one** example, how indirect aggression could improve performance in a sport. (Grade 5-7)

Indirect aggression could be used during a tennis serve to allow a player ....
to aim their aggression at the ball to hit it powerfully across the court. ....

[2 marks]

Exam Questions

1   Which **one** of these examples requires a low arousal level? (Grade 1-3)

Shade **one** oval only.

A   Putting a ball in golf   ⬭

B   Jumping to block a shot in volleyball   ⬭

C   Tackling an opponent in rugby   ⬭

D   Sprinting in a 100 m race   ⬭

[1 mark]

2   Which **one** of these characteristics is most associated with introverts? (Grade 1-3)

Shade **one** oval only.

A   Enjoys interaction with others   ⬭

B   Very talkative   ⬭

C   Often thoughtful   ⬭

D   Easily bored when alone   ⬭

[1 mark]

3   **Figure 1** is an incomplete graph of the inverted-U theory. (Grade 3-5)

Complete **Figure 1** by sketching the shape of the inverted-U theory.
Label the axes with arousal level and performance level.

> You could be asked to describe the inverted-U theory in words.

Figure 1

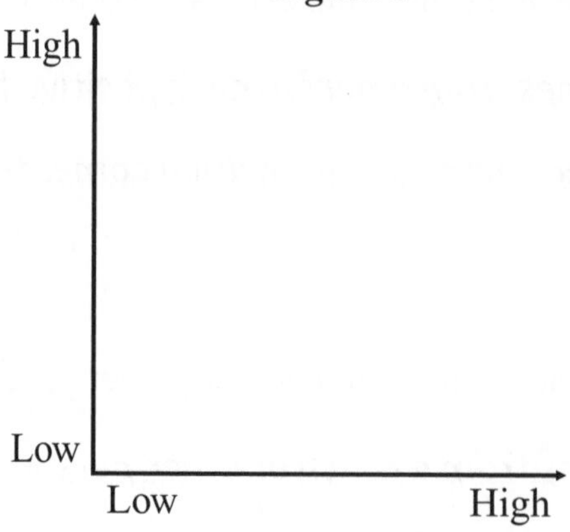

High

Low

Low   High

[2 marks]

4   Katarina is an elite level hammer thrower training for the Olympic Games. (Grade 5-7)

Explain why 'knowledge of performance' feedback would be effective feedback for Katarina.

....

....

....

....

[2 marks]

Exam Questions

5   Stress management techniques can benefit performance.

   (a) Name **two** stress management techniques. (Grade 3-5)

      1 ....

      2 ....

      [2 marks]

   (b) Explain, using **one** example, why a footballer may choose (Grade 5-7)
       to use a stress management technique during a game.

      ....

      ....

      ....

      [2 marks]

6   Using the stages of the information processing model,
     analyse how a footballer tackles an opponent.

     For this question, you can pick up marks by
     naming the stages of the information processing
     model and linking them to a football tackle.

   ....

   ....

   ....

   ....

   ....

   ....

   ....

   ....

   ....

   ....

   ....

   ....

   ....

   [6 marks]

Revision Summary

Knowledge
Organiser

Quick
Quiz

Time for some feedback on Sports Psychology. To check you're achieving your goals:

* Use the **Knowledge Organiser** to go over all the **key points**.
* Try an **online quiz** for a quick bit of **extra practice**.
* Tackle the **summary questions** below. Yes, they're hard — try to answer them **from memory** to **really test** how well you know the topic. The **answers** are all **in the section**, so go over anything **you're unsure of** again.

Learning Skills (p.59) ☑

1) What is a 'skill' in sport? How is 'ability' different?
2) a) Which type of skill needs lots of thought or decision-making to perform?
   b) What is the name of the type of skill on the opposite end of the continuum (or scale)?
3) What is the difference between an open and a closed skill? Give an example of each.
4) a) Which type of skill has its pace controlled by the person performing it?
   b) What about a skill where the actions of other people control how fast or when it occurs?
5) a) Which type of skill involves powerful movements by large muscle groups?
   b) What is the name of the opposite type of skill? How is it different?

Goal Setting (p.60) ☑

6) Why might a performer set themselves a goal?
7) What is the difference between performance and outcome goals?
   Why are performance goals usually better?
8) a) State what term each of the letters in SMART stands for and explain what each one means.
   b) Explain how using each of the terms in SMART would help you to achieve a goal.

Guidance and Feedback (p.63-64) ☑

9) What is verbal guidance? Why is it more suited to elite performers? What are the downsides of it?
10) What is visual guidance? Why is it effective for teaching closed skills?
    Why is it less effective for teaching complex skills to beginners?
11) What is manual guidance? What are the benefits of it?
12) What is mechanical guidance? Give two advantages to using mechanical guidance.
13) What disadvantage do manual and mechanical guidance have in common?
14) What is intrinsic feedback? How is extrinsic feedback different?
15) What is the difference between knowledge of performance and knowledge of results?
16) Explain why positive feedback can be helpful for beginners in sports.
    Explain why negative feedback can be helpful for elite athletes.
17) a) Sketch out the four stages of the information processing model.
    b) Add a few notes to each stage to explain what it means.

Mental Preparation, Emotion and Personality (p.65-66) ☑

18) List six different ways of mentally preparing for sport. Put stars next to the five of these that are stress management techniques that could help lower your arousal level.
19) Sketch the 'inverted-U graph' for arousal levels. Don't forget to label the axes.
    What does the graph show about the relationship between performance and arousal levels?
20) a) Why do some sports need lower arousal levels? What type of skills do they tend to involve?
    b) What type of skills need higher arousal levels?
21) What is the difference between intrinsic motivation and extrinsic motivation?
    Why is intrinsic motivation usually more effective?
22) How is direct aggression different to indirect aggression?
23) a) Sum up the characteristics of an introvert. What type of sports do introverts usually enjoy?
    b) What are extroverts like? And what type of sports do they usually prefer?

Influences on Participation

Participation means **taking part** in sport or other physical activities. Whether you **participate** in sports, and the **type of sports** you play, can be affected by lots of **different factors**...

People Influence the **Activities** you do

Your family and friends can have a big influence on whether you do sport, and which sports you choose.

FAMILY

- Parents might encourage their children to take up sports, or discourage them.
- If your parents or siblings play sport, or are interested in it, you're familiar with sport from a young age. You may also have more opportunities to take part.

FRIENDS

- You're influenced by the attitudes of people your own age (your peers), especially your close friends...
- For example, if all your mates play football, you're likely to play football with them. If your mates say that sport is rubbish and don't play it, you might do less sport.

ROLE MODELS

- People who excel in their sport can become role models for their sport and inspire people to be like them. This encourages more people to participate in their sport.

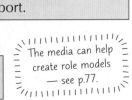
The media can help create role models — see p.77.

Your **Gender** may **Influence** whether you do an Activity

Although things are getting better, there's still a real gender divide in participation. Surveys carried out by Sport England show that, overall, fewer women participate regularly in sport than men.

- This may be because many women's events have a lower profile than men's, as they get less media coverage. This has meant that in many sports there are fewer female role models to inspire younger generations to take up the sport.
- Less media coverage also means there is less sponsorship available for women's sport, meaning there are fewer opportunities and less money for women to do sport at a high level.
- Gender tagging — outdated attitudes about some things being "women's activities" and others being "men's activities" might also affect what sports you decide to take up.
- This includes gender stereotypes about it 'not being feminine' to get sweaty or muddy, or to play sports where you need aggression. Similarly, stereotypes about masculinity may also mean boys are expected to play more aggressive sports or are mocked for enjoying activities seen as less 'manly'.

Ethnicity and Religion can have an Effect too

1) Sometimes your religious beliefs or ethnic background can influence the physical activity you do.

   E.g. many Muslim women keep their bodies covered up. This may mean they're less likely to participate in activities such as swimming because of the clothing that's expected to be worn.

2) Religious festivals and days may impact on when you can play sport. For example, some Christians won't play sport on a Sunday because it's the Sabbath, so could not join a Sunday league team.

3) Racism and racial abuse used to be a huge problem in sport. Campaigns such as the Kick It Out campaign have helped to raise awareness of the problem. Also, punishments for players and fans who are racist are now much more severe than they used to be.

4) Governing bodies have also tried to help create more positive role models to inspire and engage younger generations to participate.

5) Policies like the 'Rooney Rule' in American football, which says that teams must interview at least one ethnic minority candidate for any head coaching job, are also helping to create more opportunities.

Influences on Participation

Another page of **influences on participation** — so many influences, so little time... **Disability** can influence what activities you do, and so can your **job**, where you **live** and how much **money** you have...

Disability can Influence how Active you are

1) Having a <u>disability</u> can limit the physical activities you can do. Studies show that participation rates for disabled people are lower than they are for non-disabled people.

2) The <u>opportunities</u> in sport and <u>access to sporting facilities</u> for disabled people used to be few and far between.

3) Nowadays, there are many <u>schemes</u> set up to give disabled people <u>more opportunities</u> to exercise and take part in activities within their physical limits. These schemes focus on:

Adapting sports so that they're more accessible for disabled people — e.g. wheelchair basketball or handcycling.	**Creating new sports** specifically for disabled people — like boccia (a game like bowls that can be played from a wheelchair) and goalball (a game like handball that blind people can play).

Including disabled people in activities alongside non-disabled people. This helps to <u>challenge stereotypes</u> about disabled people as well as giving disabled people the <u>opportunity</u> to enjoy a <u>wide range</u> of activities.

4) Disabled sporting events are now given a lot more <u>media coverage</u> than they once were. The Paralympics now gets extensive <u>media coverage</u>, like the Olympics.

5) This media coverage is helping to <u>change people's attitudes</u> towards disability and sport.

6) It's also helping create many more <u>disabled role models</u> (like <u>Dame Tanni Grey-Thompson</u> and <u>Ellie Simmonds</u>), which encourages more disabled people to get active.

Your Socio-Economic Group can also have an Effect

1) <u>Socio-economic groups</u> are just a <u>fancy</u> way of grouping people based on how much <u>money</u> they have, where they <u>live</u> and the type of <u>job</u> they do.

> "<u>Working class</u>", "<u>middle class</u>" and "<u>young professional</u>" are all examples of socio-economic groups.

2) Studies seem to show that, in general, people in <u>lower socio-economic groups</u> are <u>less likely</u> to regularly take part in sport. The <u>kinds</u> of activities people do can also be affected by their socio-economic group.

- Most sports cost <u>money</u>. This means that some people can't <u>afford</u> to take part.
- Lots of sports — like <u>horse riding</u>, <u>skiing</u>, <u>sailing</u> and even <u>cycling</u> — require specialist <u>equipment</u> and <u>clothing</u>. This can be very <u>expensive</u>, so could prevent people from taking part.
- Some sports require special <u>facilities</u> — like <u>ski slopes</u> or <u>ice rinks</u>. If you don't live in an <u>area</u> with these sorts of facilities, you won't easily be able to <u>do</u> those sports.
- If you don't have access to a <u>car</u> or good <u>public transport</u> to get to the facilities, this makes it a lot harder to participate. You'll be more likely to do a <u>more accessible</u> sport like football or basketball.
- If you work <u>shifts</u> or <u>irregular hours</u> it can be hard to join clubs or groups that meet in the evenings or at the weekend.
- Playing sport can also require a lot of <u>free time</u>. If you <u>work long hours</u>, or have <u>family commitments</u> like caring for children, you might just <u>not</u> have the <u>time</u>.

We're all under the influence...

There really are a lot of different factors that influence whether or not someone takes part in physical activity. Make sure you learn all of the ones covered on the last two pages. And, as if that wasn't enough, there are still more factors to learn on the next page... Keep at it though, you're nearly there.

Influences on Participation

That's right, it's another page covering influences on participation. There are just **two more factors** for you to learn, then you've got some **data on participation rates** to look forward to.

Age can Limit the Activities you can do

1) Some sports are more <u>popular</u> than others with different age groups.

2) Most people aged 16-30 have <u>loads of choice</u> for physical activity.

3) People over 50 are more <u>physically limited</u> in the sports they can choose. They tend to do <u>less strenuous</u> activities like walking or swimming.

4) Some sports, such as <u>weightlifting</u> or <u>endurance events</u>, can potentially <u>damage</u> a <u>young person's</u> body. Competitions in these sorts of activities often have a <u>minimum age restriction</u>.

5) Young people often have more <u>spare time</u> to do sport. As people get <u>older</u> and have <u>careers</u> and <u>families</u>, there's <u>less time</u> available for playing sport.

PE in Schools can have a big effect on Participation

PE in schools plays a big <u>role</u> in shaping people's <u>feelings</u> towards <u>sport</u> and <u>exercise</u>:

PE CLASSES

<u>PE classes</u> and <u>after-school activities</u> are a way for students to try out lots of different sports. This allows students to become <u>familiar</u> with lots of activities, which might encourage regular participation. It's really important that schools offer a <u>wide range</u> of activities, so there's something for everyone. This will encourage more students to join in and enjoy sport:

- Some students are put off by PE at school because they find it <u>awkward</u> or <u>embarrassing</u>.

- Allowing students to <u>choose</u> what activities they would like to do, and listening to students' suggestions about improving PE, can make students <u>more willing</u> to take part.

- Some students do not enjoy the <u>competitive</u> nature of sport, so offering <u>non-competitive activities</u> in PE is a good idea — e.g. fitness classes or yoga.

PE TEACHER

Having a really good PE <u>teacher</u>, or sports coach at a club, can really help to <u>inspire</u> people too. The flip side of this is that a <u>bad experience</u> in PE could end up <u>putting you off</u> sports and exercise.

FACILITIES

The <u>facilities</u> a school has available can <u>limit</u> what activities it can offer. Also, grimy old <u>changing rooms</u> and <u>equipment</u> can mean some students just aren't <u>inspired</u> to <u>join in</u> with PE at all.

You might have to Interpret Data about Participation Rates

You might be asked to <u>analyse graphs</u> showing participation rates for different sports and activities.

1) You may get asked to <u>compare activities</u>, e.g. to say which activity has <u>increased</u> or <u>decreased</u> most from one point to another.

2) The <u>bigger</u> the <u>difference</u> between these <u>two points</u>, the <u>bigger</u> the <u>increase</u> or <u>decrease</u>.

3) For example, the graph on the right shows that:

- Participation in <u>swimming</u> <u>decreased</u> more than running or cycling from <u>17/18</u> to <u>18/19</u>.

- Participation in <u>cycling increased</u> more than swimming or running from <u>18/19</u> to <u>19/20</u>.

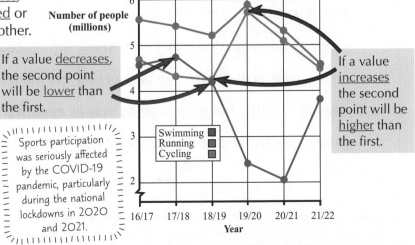

Graph showing the number of English people aged 16 or over who participated at least twice in the previous 28 days, between 2016 and 2022.

If a value <u>decreases</u>, the second point will be <u>lower</u> than the first.

If a value <u>increases</u> the second point will be <u>higher</u> than the first.

Sports participation was seriously affected by the COVID-19 pandemic, particularly during the national lockdowns in 2020 and 2021.

Warm-Up and Worked Exam Questions

There are so many things that can influence whether or not you participate in sport it's tough to remember all of them. Test yourself with these questions to check you've got all the details stored in your memory.

Warm-Up Questions

1) How can your family influence whether you play sport?
2) How can role models improve participation rates?
3) Give one way that your religious beliefs might affect the sports you do.
4) Give one way of providing more opportunities for disabled people to participate in sport.
5) What is meant by socio-economic group?
6) Give two ways that school PE lessons might influence your attitude towards exercise.

Worked Exam Questions

1 Outline **one** way that schools can encourage students to enjoy sport and physical activity. Grade 1-3

.A school could allow students to choose from a range of activities.........................

There are loads of answers you could give, but you only need to put one to get the mark.

[1 mark]

2 Explain how age can limit the level of participation in certain sports. Grade 3-5
Use an example in your answer.

Some sports place the body under a lot of strain, which makes them unsuitable for......

children or older people. For example, children should not participate in weightlifting,.

as their bodies are not developed enough to withstand it. Similarly, weightlifting........

would not be an appropriate sport for the elderly, as the risk of injury will be too high..

[3 marks]

3 Discuss possible influences that may affect women's participation in physical activity. Grade 5-7

Women's participation may be positively influenced by media coverage of sporting.....

events, which can create female sporting role models and inspire women to take part in

physical activity. However, women may be negatively influenced by gender stereotypes

and not participate in traditionally 'male' sports because of sexist attitudes.................

[3 marks]

 You're asked to discuss the influences, so you need to think about both positive and negative influences.

Exam Questions

1   Which **one** of these is a socio-economic influence
    on whether someone participates in sport?   (Grade 1-3)

    Shade **one** oval only.

    A   Sexism   ⬭
    B   Religious beliefs   ⬭
    C   Cost   ⬭
    D   Racism   ⬭

    [1 mark]

2   Studies show that participation rates in physical activity and sport
    are lower for disabled people than they are for non-disabled people.   (Grade 3-5)

    Suggest **two** possible reasons for the lower participation rates amongst disabled people.

    1 ....

    ....

    2 ....

    ....

    [2 marks]

3   Jake is a primary school student. He doesn't participate in any sport outside of school.

    Identify potential reasons for Jake's lack of participation in sport. Justify your choices.

    ....

    ....

    ....

    ....

    ....

    ....

    ....

    ....

    ....

    ....

    [6 marks]

Commercialisation of Sport

Lots of people are raking in cash from sport these days. This is the **commercialisation** of sport, and the next three pages are all about it. Lots of this money comes from **the media** and through **sponsorship**.

Commercialisation Means Making Money

- The commercialisation of sport means managing sport in a way designed to make profit — mostly through sponsorship and the media.

- Sponsorship is the provision of money, equipment, clothing/footwear or facilities to an individual, team or event in return for some financial gain.

- The media (e.g. television companies, radio broadcasters and newspapers) pay so they can cover the sport, which means people will buy their newspaper or watch their TV show. Some companies sell sport on TV, or over the internet, as a subscription package too.

- Broadcasting sports on television and the Internet means it now reaches an even larger, global audience — this is known as the globalisation of sport. This all makes sponsorship even more valuable.

- Social media gives fans new ways to see their favourite sports stars and further promotes sponsors.

You can Interpret Data About Commercialisation

There's lots of data to do with commercialisation of sport, so here's an example and how you can interpret it:

1) The graph on the right shows the total amount spent each year on shirt sponsorship (that's companies paying to have their logo on the front of a team's shirt) in the Premier League.

2) The graph shows that every year, spending on shirt sponsorship in the Premier League has increased (there is an "upward trend").

3) If the graph carried on past 2019, you'd expect it to generally keep on going upwards.

4) You can also see that the biggest increase in spending was from 2016 to 2017 — shown by the line going up more steeply.

5) The smallest increase in spending was from 2015 to 2016 — the line between these years is more shallow.

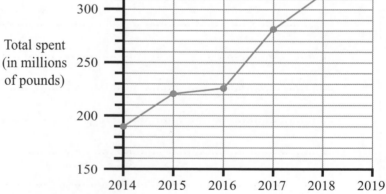

A graph showing the amount spent on front-of-shirt sponsorship in the Premier League between 2014 and 2019.

Total spent (in millions of pounds)

Year season began

Show me the money...

It's really important that you understand what sponsorship is and why companies pay so much money to do it. The media is another key player in the commercialisation of sport. Make sure you know why, then it's on to the next page for more info on how sport, the media and sponsorship are all connected.

Commercialisation of Sport

This page covers the **links** between **sport**, **the media** and **sponsorship** in more detail.
This can be quite tricky, so take your time and read through each of the boxes below really carefully.

Sport, the Media and Sponsorship are all Connected

Sport, the media and sponsorship have grown to depend on one another. There are advantages and disadvantages to this relationship for the sponsor, the sport, the players, the spectators and the officials.

SPONSORSHIP AND SPORT

1) Sponsorship deals mean companies can associate their name with the prestige of successful sportspeople and teams. This is an effective form of advertising, which helps the sponsor to make more money.

2) These deals mean big money for sport — which can be spent on development, e.g. of a new stadium or facilities. This benefits the players and the spectators. This money can also pay for technology to help officials (see p.79).

3) Sponsorship money also means players and officials can be paid good wages, and players can train full-time. This benefits everyone, because they will perform better.

THE MEDIA AND SPORT

1) The media pay for the rights to cover sporting events, which provides investment for sports to develop at lower levels.

2) Media coverage makes more people aware of the sport, so more people may play it or watch it.

3) Media coverage of elite players and athletes can create role models who inspire people to play.

4) This can make players into superstars. But the downside is that players are hounded by the media and their private lives are all over the news.

5) Also, the media can hold so much power over sport that they'll change things:

   • The number of games played, or the timings of matches, might be changed so more matches can be shown. This risks injury to players through lack of rest, and might mean spectators miss a game because it's not at a convenient time.

   • Also, rules may be changed — e.g. the tiebreaker set was brought into tennis to make matches shorter.

6) Being able to watch on TV or the Internet, rather than going to the game, can save fans money. However, fewer fans buying tickets means losses in ticket sales for the sport and a poorer atmosphere at the stadium for spectators.

7) The media's analysis of refereeing decisions puts sports officials under a lot of pressure.

8) Media analysis of games can also educate spectators, so they understand the sport better.

SPONSORSHIP AND THE MEDIA

1) The more media coverage a sport gets, the more people watch it. This makes sponsorship more valuable, as it can reach a larger audience.

2) This increases the likelihood of sponsorship and means the sport and players can demand more money for their sponsorship deals.

Page 77 was brought to you in collaboration with CGP...

Companies provide sponsorship for big sporting events, such as the Netball World Cup. Write down one way in which sponsorship might affect: the sport, players, spectators and officials.

Commercialisation of Sport

Sponsorship can be a little complicated. You need to know that it has its **downsides** and that not all types of sponsor are **suitable**. Read on to find out about the **dark side** of sponsorship...

Sponsorship **Isn't** All Great

There can be drawbacks to sponsorship for <u>teams</u> and <u>individuals</u>:

1) Sometimes, the money is only available for the <u>top players</u> and teams, so benefits the <u>elite</u> — <u>not</u> the <u>sport</u> as a <u>whole</u>.

2) It could all turn nasty — if an athlete gets <u>injured</u>, loses their <u>form</u> or gets a <u>bad reputation</u> they could lose their sponsorship deal. <u>Bad behaviour</u> by an <u>athlete</u> reflects badly on the <u>sponsor</u> too and could <u>damage</u> the company's <u>reputation</u>.

3) Sometimes athletes have to fulfil <u>contracts</u> with their sponsor — they might have to turn up at a <u>special event</u> or appear in a <u>TV advert</u> (even if they don't want to).

4) Athletes can get into <u>trouble</u> with their sponsor if they're spotted using <u>another company</u>'s products.

5) If a team really <u>needs</u> a sponsor's money, this puts the sponsor in a position of <u>power</u>. This means they can <u>influence</u> the team's playing style or team selection.

6) In some sports where there are breaks in play, <u>adverts</u> will be shown. The game won't be allowed to <u>restart</u> until the advert break is <u>finished</u>, which can be quite <u>boring</u> for <u>spectators</u> in the stadium.

One bad story can mean the end for an athlete's sponsorship deals...

Some Sponsors are **Inappropriate**

Sponsorship brings in loads of money, but you have to be careful not to <u>promote</u> the <u>wrong</u> image, especially in <u>youth</u> sports:

- <u>Cigarette</u> and <u>tobacco</u> companies aren't allowed to sponsor sports in the UK. This is because their products are <u>harmful</u> and <u>unhealthy</u>.

- <u>Alcoholic drinks</u> companies are allowed to sponsor some sports, but this can be <u>bad</u> as it gives alcohol a <u>false image of health</u>. The same is true for <u>unhealthy food</u> companies.

- Also, as sport is watched by <u>children</u>, advertising alcohol and fast food could be <u>encouraging</u> young people to <u>drink</u> or <u>eat unhealthily</u>.

In the past, it was common for cigarette companies to sponsor sporting events and teams. Nowadays, this is seen as unacceptable.

EXAM TIP

Sponsorship — sometimes it comes at a price...

If you get a question about the impact of sponsorship in the exam, you'll need to weigh up the <u>pros and cons</u>, especially when it comes to fast-food and alcohol companies. Also, make sure to take note of the <u>age group</u> mentioned in the question — for example, it might be okay for an alcohol company to sponsor an adult event, but not to sponsor a youth one.

Technology in Sport

There's loads of **technology** used in sport — make sure you learn all about it for the exam.

Technology can help Players to Perform Better

1) Lots of the technology used today is designed to help athletes perform better at their sports. This benefits spectators as well as performers, as new levels of sporting excellence are achieved.

2) New materials are used to make sports equipment and clothes more effective — from shoes to swimming costumes to tennis rackets. This helps players reach new levels of performance.

3) Improvements to training facilities, like all-weather pitches, mean that training doesn't have to stop for bad weather. This means more time can be spent training, so performances will improve.

4) There have also been developments to make sports safer, like better protective clothing and better playing surfaces. Also, medical technology can help athletes recover from injuries quickly and safely.

5) Video footage and 3D modelling software can be used by coaches to analyse an athlete's movement. This can be done to a very high degree of accuracy, so an athlete's technique can be fine-tuned. In events like the 100 m sprint, where winning may come down to a few milliseconds, this level of accuracy is really important.

6) All this technology is expensive though. This can mean that only people with lots of money can compete at the highest level.

7) There is a worry that technology can give athletes an unfair advantage over their competitors. If sport becomes less about the abilities of the athletes and more about the technology they're using, it kind of stops being interesting for spectators.

Technology can help Officials to make Correct Decisions

Many sports now make use of technology during matches to help referees and umpires.

1) Hawk-Eye is a company that uses optical tracking technology to track the path and spin of balls, as well as the athlete's skeleton during play in multiple sports to ensure that officiating decisions are accurate and fair, most notably in tennis and football.

2) Decision Review System (DRS) (cricket) — players are allowed to challenge an umpire's decision and have it reviewed by the third umpire, who uses various bits of technology (including Hawk-Eye) to decide whether the on-field umpire was correct or not.

3) Television Match Official (TMO) (rugby union) — the TMO is an extra official who watches video replays. The referee on the pitch can consult with the TMO to help them make key decisions.

4) Goal-line technology (football) — there are cameras pointed at each goal that are used to tell whether or not the ball has crossed the goal line.

ADVANTAGES

- All these systems help to make the sport more fair, which benefits spectators and players by avoiding the frustration of wrong decisions.
- They help officials to make valid and reliable decisions, even in marginal situations. This lessens the pressure on them.
- The DRS in cricket has shown that the umpires are right most of the time. This has led to increased respect for umpires.
- Sponsors can use the breaks in play that some of these technologies cause to show adverts.

DISADVANTAGES

- These systems are expensive to install, so are only used at the top end of sporting leagues.
- The fact that things can be reviewed could undermine the authority of the officials on the pitch. This could lead to players contesting every decision the referee makes.
- Referring to a video replay can sometimes take a long time. Some people worry that these breaks disrupt the flow of play and can also be boring for spectators.

Warm-Up and Worked Exam Questions

Both the commercialisation of sport and the use of technology can affect performers, officials, spectators and sponsors in lots of ways. Time to test how well you can remember them all with some questions.

Warm-Up Questions

1) What is meant by the commercialisation of sport?
2) Name three different types of media that feature sport.
3) Media coverage can only have a positive impact on sport. True or false?
4) Give one possible reason why a company may sponsor a performer.
5) Give one possible disadvantage of sponsorship for a performer.
6) Why might a tobacco or alcohol company be an unsuitable sponsor for a sports team?
7) How can improvements in technology help a performer to avoid injury?
8) Give one disadvantage of technology in sport for a spectator.

Worked Exam Questions

1 Complete **Table 1** with **one** advantage and **one** disadvantage of sponsorship for sport as a whole. Grade 3-5

Table 1

Advantage	Disadvantage
Sponsorship brings in lots of money that can be spent on developing sports.	The money brought in through sponsorship may only benefit elite performers and not sport as a whole.

[2 marks]

2 Hawk-Eye optical tracking technology can be used in tennis to track the path of the ball. Performers can challenge the official's decision of whether the ball is in or out. Grade 5-7

Discuss the impact of using Hawk-Eye technology during a tennis match.

Hawk-Eye can help officials to make valid and reliable decisions, especially in
situations where it's difficult to tell whether the ball is in or out. However, it could
undermine the authority of officials by encouraging players to question every
decision that the umpire makes. Hawk-Eye could help to make the match more fair,
which benefits spectators and players by avoiding the frustration of wrong decisions.
However, challenges can disrupt the flow of play, which might irritate spectators.

[4 marks]

> You can't get all four marks if you only give positive (or negative) effects of Hawk-Eye, so make sure you consider both.

Exam Questions

1   Which **one** of these is **not** a typical form of sponsorship
    that an individual or team would receive?   (Grade 1-3)

    Shade **one** oval only.

    A   Money   ⬭
    B   Holidays   ⬭
    C   Equipment   ⬭
    D   Facilities   ⬭

    [1 mark]

2   Outline what the commercialisation of sport is and ⟵ With this question, you need to make
    evaluate the impact it has on performers and spectators.   sure you weigh up the good and
                                                               bad sides of the commercialisation of
                                                               sport for performers and spectators.

    ....

    ....

    ....

    ....

    ....

    ....

    ....

    ....

    ....

    ....

    ....

    ....

    ....

    ....

    ....

    ....

    ....

    ....

    ....

    [9 marks]

Sporting Behaviour

This page is about good and bad **behaviour** in sport. Make sure you learn the definitions below — **sportsmanship** is **good** sporting behaviour and **gamesmanship** is behaviour that seems **unfair**.

Sportsmanship is About Being Fair and Humble

Being a good sportsperson is <u>more</u> than just playing by the rules. You also have to show good 'sportsmanship' (even if you lose) and <u>uphold</u> the 'contract to compete'.

> **Sportsmanship** means playing <u>within the rules</u>, upholding the <u>spirit of the game</u> and using <u>sports etiquette</u>.

> The <u>contract to compete</u> is an unwritten <u>agreement</u> between competitors to <u>comply</u> with all the rules (both <u>written</u> and <u>unwritten</u>) and to do their best.

1) Good sportsmanship means no <u>rubbing it in</u> the opposition's face if you <u>win</u>. And no going <u>off in a huff</u> if you <u>lose</u>.

2) It also means observing the <u>etiquette</u> of an activity.

> <u>Sporting etiquette</u> means following the <u>unwritten rules</u> and <u>conventions</u> of the activity.

<u>Etiquette</u> is <u>not</u> a list of <u>enforceable rules</u> (i.e. players <u>can't</u> be <u>punished</u> for poor etiquette), but it is usually <u>observed</u>. Here are some examples...

- In cricket, a batsman might choose to '<u>walk</u>' if they think they've been caught <u>out</u> — even if the umpire has <u>ruled</u> them <u>not out</u>.
- In football, players will kick the ball <u>out of play</u> if a member of the other team goes down <u>injured</u>.
- Players <u>shake hands</u> with <u>officials</u> and <u>opponents</u> after a match, <u>regardless</u> of the outcome.
- In cycling, if someone has a <u>mechanical problem</u> with their bike (like a puncture), the other riders will <u>not</u> take advantage by <u>speeding up</u> until the problem is <u>fixed</u>.

Gamesmanship is a type of Poor Behaviour

> <u>Gamesmanship</u> is gaining an advantage by using tactics that <u>push</u> the rules <u>without breaking them</u>.

<u>Gamesmanship</u> is <u>not</u> actually cheating — but it can come <u>quite close</u>. A lot of the techniques are about <u>breaking</u> up the <u>flow</u> of a game, or <u>distracting</u> your opponents:

- <u>Time-wasting</u> in football is when players deliberately <u>faff about</u>. This <u>runs down</u> the <u>clock</u> and <u>breaks up</u> the <u>flow</u> of the game.
- In tennis, some players make loud <u>grunting</u> or <u>shrieking</u> noises when they <u>hit the ball</u> to try and <u>intimidate</u> or <u>distract</u> their opponent.
- In basketball, a manager might call a <u>timeout</u> just as the opposition win a <u>free throw</u>. This is to try and make them <u>overthink</u> the shot.

1) <u>Gamesmanship</u> does <u>not</u> normally result in <u>punishment</u> for the players, although if it is taken <u>too far</u> referees might get <u>involved</u>.

2) Using <u>performance-enhancing drugs</u> (see next page), deliberately <u>fouling</u> an opponent or being <u>violent</u> and <u>aggressive</u> are <u>not</u> gamesmanship — they all go <u>against</u> the moral values or laws of the sport.

Sportsmanship's the good one, gamesmanship's the bad one...
I know, it's easy to get confused between sportsmanship and gamesmanship. Just remember that <u>sportsmanship</u> is about 'being a good <u>sport</u>', and you can't go wrong.

Performance-Enhancing Drugs

Some people **cheat** by taking **drugs**. Drugs can help them **perform better**, but they can also cause serious **health problems**. You need to know the **positive** and **negative** effects of these drugs on the performer...

Performance-Enhancing Drugs can Improve Performance

1) Some performers use drugs to <u>improve</u> their performance and be more <u>successful</u> in their sport, which can lead to <u>wealth</u> and <u>fame</u>. Some performers also claim they use drugs to <u>level the playing field</u> — if other competitors use drugs, you're at a disadvantage unless you use them too.

2) The use of these drugs in sport is usually <u>banned</u>, and they can have <u>nasty side effects</u>. Being caught using these drugs can lead to <u>fines</u>, <u>disqualification</u> or lengthy <u>bans</u> for cheating.

3) Unfortunately, some performers still <u>break the rules</u> by taking them anyway — even with the <u>risks</u> to their <u>health</u> and <u>reputation</u> and to the <u>reputation</u> and <u>credibility</u> of their <u>sport</u> if they're caught. These are the drugs you need to know about:

Anabolic steroids are a type of anabolic agent.

ANABOLIC AGENTS

- Mimic the male sex hormone <u>testosterone</u>.
- Testosterone <u>increases</u> your <u>bone</u> and <u>muscle growth</u>, so you can get bigger and stronger, but also more <u>aggressive</u>.
- Help with <u>faster</u> recovery from exercise and are commonly taken by <u>sprinters</u>.

But...

- They can cause <u>high blood pressure</u>, <u>heart disease</u> and <u>infertility</u>, and can increase the risk of developing <u>cancer</u>.
- Women may grow <u>facial</u> and <u>body hair</u>.

DIURETICS

- Increase the amount you <u>urinate</u>, causing <u>weight loss</u> — which is beneficial if you're competing in a certain <u>weight division</u> (e.g. as in <u>boxing</u> or <u>judo</u>).

But...

- They can cause <u>cramp</u>, <u>dehydration</u>, <u>loss of salts</u>, <u>muscle weakness</u> and <u>heart damage</u>.

NARCOTIC ANALGESICS

- <u>Kill pain</u> — so injuries and fatigue, e.g. from overtraining, don't affect performance and training so much.

But...

- They're <u>addictive</u>, with unpleasant <u>withdrawal symptoms</u>.
- Feeling less pain can make an athlete train <u>too hard</u>, causing <u>overtraining</u>.
- They can lead to <u>constipation</u> and <u>low blood pressure</u>.

PEPTIDE HORMONES (EPO)

- Cause the production of other <u>hormones</u> — similar to anabolic agents.
- <u>EPO</u> (Erythropoietin) is a peptide hormone that causes the body to produce more red blood cells. This <u>increases oxygen-carrying capacity</u> and <u>endurance</u>, which benefits, e.g. <u>road racing cyclists</u>.

But...

- They can cause <u>strokes</u>, <u>heart problems</u>, <u>abnormal growth</u> and <u>diabetes</u>.

STIMULANTS

- Affect the <u>central nervous system</u> (the bits of your brain and spine that control your <u>reactions</u>).
- They can <u>increase mental</u> and <u>physical alertness</u>.

But...

- They can lead to <u>high blood pressure</u>, <u>heart</u> and <u>liver problems</u>, and <u>strokes</u>.
- They're <u>addictive</u>.

BETA BLOCKERS

- <u>Reduce heart rate</u>, <u>muscle tension</u>, <u>blood pressure</u> and the effect of <u>adrenaline</u>. This <u>steadies shaking hands</u>, which improves <u>fine motor skills</u>.
- This <u>calming</u>, <u>relaxing</u> effect is beneficial in e.g. <u>shooting sports</u>.

But...

- They can cause <u>nausea</u>, <u>weakness</u>, <u>cramp</u> and <u>heart failure</u>.
- They're <u>banned</u> in some sports and if allowed must be <u>prescribed</u> by a <u>medical professional</u>.

Blood Doping Increases Red Blood Cell Count

1) Blood doping increases the number of <u>red blood cells</u> in the bloodstream. This increases <u>oxygen supply</u> to the muscles and <u>improves</u> performance and endurance.

2) The increase in <u>cardiovascular endurance</u> can benefit athletes such as <u>long-distance runners</u> and <u>cyclists</u>.

3) One method of blood doping involves <u>removing</u> some blood from an athlete several weeks before a competition. The blood is <u>frozen</u>, then <u>re-injected</u> before the athlete competes.

4) Possible side effects of injecting red blood cells include <u>blood thickening</u> (viscosity), <u>infections</u>, <u>increased risk of heart attack</u> and <u>blocked blood vessels</u> (embolism).

Blood doping is banned but can be hard to test for.

Spectator Behaviour

Big sporting events draw big **crowds** — this has both advantages and disadvantages.
Make sure you learn what these are and also what can be done to **prevent hooliganism**.

Spectators create an Atmosphere

1) <u>Crowds</u> at sporting events create an <u>atmosphere</u> and this adds to the <u>excitement</u>, making the event more enjoyable for <u>spectators</u> and <u>players</u>.

2) Also, this can create a '<u>home-field advantage</u>' — the 'home' team <u>perform better</u> because they're in <u>familiar surroundings</u> with more fans supporting them. This can also <u>intimidate</u> the <u>opposition</u>.

3) However, sometimes all those spectators can put <u>pressure</u> on the performers, who end up performing worse because they are <u>nervous</u> and <u>afraid</u> to make <u>mistakes</u>.

4) Having spectators at sporting events for <u>younger people</u> (like youth leagues in football) can put more <u>pressure</u> on the kids who are taking part. This can <u>discourage</u> children from taking up activities, so can negatively affect <u>participation rates</u> (see pages 71-73).

5) At big events, it takes a lot of <u>planning</u> and <u>money</u> to make sure spectators are <u>safe</u>. With large groups there's the chance of <u>crowd trouble</u> and <u>hooliganism</u>...

Hooliganism is when fans Become Aggressive

Hooliganism is <u>rowdy</u>, <u>aggressive</u> and sometimes <u>violent behaviour</u> of fans and spectators of sport. You need to know what <u>causes</u> hooliganism and how it can be <u>prevented</u>...

CAUSES

1) <u>Rivalries</u> between fans. These rivalries might be <u>built up</u> by the <u>press</u> and the <u>media</u> so they seem even more <u>important</u>. This <u>hype</u> can cause fans to take the match too <u>seriously</u>.

2) Some fans might have been <u>drinking</u>, or even taking <u>drugs</u>, which can fuel <u>aggression</u> and <u>violence</u>.

3) <u>Frustration</u> with decisions made by <u>officials</u>, or just frustration with how the <u>match</u> is <u>going</u>, can lead to spectators getting <u>angry</u>.

4) Some people see hooliganism as a <u>display of masculinity</u>, or a way of fans proving themselves to be <u>macho</u>. <u>Peer pressure</u> can make people feel they <u>have to join in</u>. There could also be a '<u>gang mentality</u>', where people feel <u>less responsible</u> for their <u>actions</u> because they're in a <u>group</u>.

METHODS OF PREVENTION

1) <u>Kick-offs</u> can be made <u>earlier</u> for games where it's likely there will be trouble. This leaves <u>less time</u> between the <u>pubs</u> opening and the <u>start</u> of the game, so fans will be less <u>drunk</u> during the game. <u>Alcohol restrictions</u> can also be brought in to control buying alcohol <u>within</u> the stadium.

   • However, fans often get round this by <u>drinking more</u> before they go to the game.
     Also, having <u>earlier kick-offs</u> can make it inconvenient for <u>travelling fans</u> to get to the game.

2) Making every stadium '<u>all-seated</u>' so fans don't have to stand. This is <u>safer</u> because people are <u>less packed together</u>. It's also easier for <u>stewards</u> and <u>police</u> to get to <u>troublemakers</u>.

3) Fans can be <u>segregated</u> (sat in separate sections) to stop <u>fighting</u> inside the ground. Sometimes home and away fans <u>enter</u> and <u>leave</u> the ground at <u>different times</u>.

   • This doesn't help prevent violence <u>outside</u> of the stadium though, and it can mean it takes longer for fans to get into or out of the stadium, which is annoying for the fans.

4) The <u>number</u> of <u>police</u> and <u>stewards</u> at games can be increased, which boosts <u>security</u> in the ground. Also, <u>video surveillance</u> and other <u>technology</u> can be used to monitor crowds.

   • It can be very <u>expensive</u> to install all this technology and pay extra police and stewards.

5) For fans who have committed hooliganism in the <u>past</u>, there are <u>banning orders</u> and <u>travel restrictions</u>, e.g. confiscating passports. This means that the <u>worst offenders</u> aren't at games.

6) There have been lots of <u>campaigns</u> to <u>educate</u> fans about the <u>harm</u> that's <u>caused</u> by hooliganism.

Warm-Up and Worked Exam Questions

There's a wide range of topics covered in the last few pages. Use this page of questions to check you've got it all, then go back and re-read anything you're stuck on before trying the exam questions on the next page.

Warm-Up Questions

1) What is the difference between gamesmanship and sportsmanship?
2) Give one example of sporting etiquette.
3) Deliberately fouling an opponent is an example of gamesmanship. True or false?
4) Give one positive effect and one negative effect of using anabolic agents.
5) Why might a performer use narcotic analgesics?
6) Outline what the peptide hormone 'EPO (Erythropoietin)' does.
   Which type of performer would benefit from using EPO?
7) List two advantages for the home team of having a large crowd at a football match.
8) Describe how all-seater stadia may help to prevent hooliganism.

Worked Exam Questions

1   Define the **contract to compete**.

> The contract to compete is an agreement between competitors to comply
> with both the written and unwritten rules of the sport, and to do their best.

[1 mark]

2   Hooliganism is when spectators of sport become aggressive.

(a) Outline **three** reasons why hooliganism occurs.

> 1 There might be rivalries between groups of fans.
>
> 2 The media might create a hype, which can cause fans to become rowdy.
>
> 3 Fans might have been drinking or taking drugs, which can fuel aggression.

[3 marks]

(b) Evaluate the use of early kick-offs as a method of preventing hooliganism.

> Early kick-offs mean there is less time for fans to drink at pubs or bars before the
>
> game, so it should help to reduce rowdy behaviour. However, it cannot prevent
>
> fans from drinking at home before the game, so may not be entirely effective.
>
> If fans have already decided before the game to cause trouble, the kick-off time
>
> won't influence their actions.

[3 marks]

 Evaluating means judging whether the use of early kick-offs is effective or not.

Exam Questions

1   Which **one** of these is an example of sporting etiquette?   (Grade 1-3)

   Shade **one** oval only.

   A   Trying to distract an opponent by grunting or shrieking in tennis   ◯

   B   Shaking hands with opponents and officials after a match   ◯

   C   Time-wasting in football   ◯

   D   Showing off to your opponents if you win   ◯

   [1 mark]

2   Which **one** of these is **not** a strategy employed to combat hooliganism?   (Grade 1-3)

   Shade **one** oval only.

   A   Segregation of fans   ◯

   B   Improved security   ◯

   C   Increasing stadium capacity   ◯

   D   Alcohol restrictions   ◯

   [1 mark]

3   Performance-enhancing drugs (PEDs) have health risks
   but some performers still choose to use them.   (Grade 3-5)

   State **one** advantage and **one** disadvantage (other than the health risks)
   for a performer using a PED.

   ....

   ....

   ....

   [2 marks]

4   State whether EPO or anabolic agents would bring the greater
   performance gains for a shot-putter. Justify your answer.   (Grade 3-5)

   ....

   ....

   ....

   [2 marks]

Exam Questions

5 In a basketball match, a player deliberately fouls an opponent who is shooting. The coach calls a timeout just before the opponent is about to take the free throw. `Grade 5-7`

Justify which of these acts is an example of gamesmanship.

....

....

....

....

[2 marks]

6 Blood doping is a form of cheating that can improve performance.

    (a) State **two** potential negative side effects of blood doping. `Grade 1-3`

       1 ....

       2 ....

[2 marks]

    (b) Suggest **one** example of a sports performer who could benefit from blood doping. `Grade 5-7` Justify your choice.

....

....

....

[3 marks]

7 Discuss the positive and negative effects that spectators can have at sporting events. `Grade 5-7`

....

....

....

....

....

....

[4 marks]

Revision Summary

Knowledge
Organiser

Quick
Quiz

Well, that's almost the end of your participation in Sport, Society and Culture.
Before you leave, have a go at these:

- Use the **Knowledge Organiser** to go over all the **key points**.
- Try an **online quiz** for a quick bit of **extra practice**.
- Tackle the **summary questions** below. Yes, they're hard — try to answer them **from memory** to **really test** how well you know the topic. The **answers** are all **in the section**, so go over anything **you're unsure of** again.

Influences on Participation (p.71-73) ☑

1) How might the following people influence your participation in sport:
   a) family?   b) friends?   c) role models?   ☑

2) Fill in the table below for the following social factors: gender, religion, ethnicity, disability, socio-economic group, age.

Social factor	Examples of how this factor might influence participation in sport
Gender	

3) Why might school PE lessons put students off sport and exercise? How might they inspire people?   ☑

Commercialisation of Sport (p.76-78) ☑

4) What does 'commercialisation' mean?   ☑

5) What is 'sponsorship'?   ☑

6) What different types of media are there?   ☑

7) For each of the following give one positive and one negative effect that increased media coverage could have on them: a) players   b) spectators   c) officials   d) the sport as a whole   ☑

8) A company decides to sponsor a sports team. Discuss the positive and negative effects that sponsorship could have on the team and on the company.   ☑

9) Why are some sponsors considered to be inappropriate?   ☑

Technology in Sport (p.79) ☑

10) Outline three ways technology can help an athlete perform better.
    What are some of the potential negative effects of technology for athletes?   ☑

11) How does technology help match officials? Are there any downsides of technology for the officials?   ☑

12) What are the pros and cons of technology for the spectators? How about for sponsors?   ☑

Sporting Behaviour and Performance-Enhancing Drugs (p.82-83) ☑

13) Give a definition and an example of: a) sportsmanship,   b) gamesmanship,   c) etiquette.   ☑

14) What is meant by the 'contract to compete'?   ☑

15) Why might performers take banned performance-enhancing drugs?
    What might the consequences be for both the performer and the sport if the performer gets caught?   ☑

16) For each of the following drugs, explain what effect it has on the body, why it might be beneficial to a sportsperson's performance and what side effects it could have: a) beta blockers   b) diuretics   c) narcotic analgesics   d) stimulants   e) anabolic agents   f) peptide hormones (EPO)   ☑

17) What is blood doping? What side effects can occur as a result of blood doping?   ☑

Spectator Behaviour (p.84) ☑

18) How can the 'home-field advantage' help a home team to perform better?   ☑

19) What negative effects can spectators have on the players?   ☑

20) What is hooliganism? Name four things that can cause hooliganism.   ☑

21) List all the strategies you know for helping to prevent hooliganism.   ☑

Health, Fitness and Well-being

Regular physical activity helps you to be **healthy** by improving your **physical**, **emotional** and **social** health and well-being. First up, the obvious one — **exercise** helps keep you **physically** healthy...

If your Body **Works Well**, you are **Physically Healthy**

See p.22 for more about how exercise benefits your body systems.

- Physical health and well-being are important parts of being healthy and happy.
- Taking part in sport or other physical activities has loads of physical benefits.

PHYSICAL HEALTH AND WELL-BEING:

1) Your body's organs, e.g. the heart, and systems, e.g. the cardiovascular system, are working well.

2) You're not suffering from any illnesses, diseases or injuries.

3) You're strong and fit enough to easily do everyday activities.

2) These positive effects on the body reduce the risk of obesity and other long-term health problems (see below). Stronger muscles and more flexible joints can make injury less likely and improve your posture. Avoiding injury also means you can continue training.

1) By exercising you can improve components of fitness (see p.33-36), which benefits your physical health:

- Aerobic exercise improves your cardiovascular endurance — your heart, blood vessels and lungs work more efficiently, so you can exercise more intensely and for longer. Your blood pressure also decreases.

- Exercise can benefit your musculo-skeletal system — muscles and bones get stronger, and joints more flexible.

- Exercise helps you to reach and maintain a healthy weight, which reduces strain on your body.

3) Physical activity makes you stronger and fitter — so everyday tasks like climbing stairs and lifting shopping are easier. This can help your emotional well-being too (see next page). It's not all good though — overtraining (see p.45) can have a negative effect on your health.

Exercise **Reduces** Risks to **Long-Term** Health

Regular physical activity can help reduce the risks of you getting certain diseases. For example:

- Regular aerobic exercise helps prevent high blood pressure by keeping your heart strong and arteries elastic, and helping to remove cholesterol from artery walls.
- This means blood can flow easily round the body, which reduces the risk of coronary heart disease (CHD), strokes and damage to your arteries.

Exercise increases levels of high density lipoprotein (HDL). HDL helps to remove cholesterol from the arteries.

Regular exercise helps prevent obesity. Exercise uses up energy, meaning that your body doesn't store it as fat (see p.91).

- Diabetes is a disease that gives you a high blood sugar level.
- Your blood sugar level is controlled by a hormone called insulin. If you have diabetes, this means you don't have enough insulin or your body's cells aren't reacting to insulin properly.
- Regular exercise helps you to maintain a healthy weight. This makes you far less likely to get diabetes.

Middle-aged and older adults have a far higher risk of diabetes, so exercise is a great way for them to lower that risk.

REVISION TASK

Regular revision exercises also have many benefits...

Health was defined way back in Section Three, so parts of this page should look a little familiar. Check you know your stuff by listing as many physical health benefits of exercise as you can.

Health, Fitness and Well-being

As well as making you physically healthy, exercise is great for your **emotional** and **social** health.
You need to be able to give examples of **how** and **why** exercise can help you **emotionally** and **socially**.

Emotional Health is about how you Feel

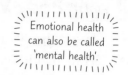
Emotional health can also be called 'mental health'.

- Being <u>healthy</u> is more than just having a body that works well — you also have to take into account how you <u>feel</u>. Your <u>emotional health</u> and <u>well-being</u> is based on how you feel about yourself and how you respond to different situations.

- Taking part in physical activity and sport can have <u>emotional benefits</u>:

EMOTIONAL HEALTH AND WELL-BEING:

1) You feel <u>content</u> and <u>confident</u> in yourself.
2) You are able to <u>manage</u> your <u>emotions</u> and <u>cope</u> with <u>challenges</u>.
3) You don't have too much <u>stress</u> or <u>anxiety</u>.
4) You're not suffering from any <u>mental illnesses</u>.

1) Physical activity can increase your <u>self-esteem</u> (your opinion of yourself) and <u>confidence</u> and generally make you <u>feel better about yourself</u>, e.g. if you feel you've achieved something. Seeing <u>improvements</u> in your <u>physical health</u>, e.g. gaining strength or improving fitness, can improve your <u>self-image</u>.

2) <u>Competing</u> against others (or yourself) can improve your ability to <u>deal</u> with <u>pressure</u> and <u>manage emotions</u>, e.g. by giving you a controlled way to channel your aggression. It's also a great way for <u>young children</u> to learn these <u>skills</u>.

3) Doing physical activity can help <u>relieve stress</u> and <u>tension</u> by taking your <u>mind off</u> whatever's worrying you and by making you feel <u>happier</u>. This helps prevent <u>stress-related illnesses</u>.

4) When you do physical activity, <u>feel good hormones</u> (like <u>serotonin</u>) are released. An <u>increased</u> level of <u>serotonin</u> in your brain may reduce your risk of developing <u>mental illnesses</u>, like <u>depression</u>.

Social Health is about how you Relate to Society

- Your <u>social health</u> and <u>well-being</u> is about how you interact with <u>others</u> and <u>form relationships</u>.
- There can be plenty of <u>social benefits</u> from doing physical activity and sport:

SOCIAL HEALTH AND WELL-BEING:

1) You have <u>friends</u>.
2) You believe you have some <u>worth</u> in society.
3) You have <u>food</u>, <u>clothing</u> and <u>shelter</u>.

1) Doing physical activity can help you <u>make friends</u> with people of different <u>ages</u> and <u>backgrounds</u>. For example, some elderly folk may have fewer opportunities to <u>socialise</u>, so sport can be a great way to make new friends. It's also a great way of <u>socialising</u> with your <u>current friends</u>.

2) By taking part in <u>team activities</u> like football, you have to practise <u>teamwork</u> — how to <u>cooperate</u> and <u>work with other people</u>. These skills are <u>useful</u> in all walks of life and can help you to be <u>successful</u>, which will increase your sense of <u>worth</u>. Being part of a team can help you to feel <u>more involved</u> in society as a whole.

3) For <u>many</u> people, physical activity probably won't put a <u>roof over their heads</u>. But the <u>skills</u> you learn through exercise and sport can help you succeed at <u>work</u> as well as at the gym or on the playing field. Being <u>physically fit</u> can also help if your job involves <u>manual labour</u> or being <u>on your feet</u> all day.

There's more to health than you might think...

These benefits are less obvious than those on the last page — especially the social health ones. But take your time and jot them down again and again until you've got them all stored away and memorised.

Sedentary Lifestyle

You've read all about the benefits of exercise, now you need to learn about the **risks** of a **sedentary lifestyle**.

A **Sedentary Lifestyle** Includes **Little Physical Activity**

1) Lifestyle choices — like how you eat and drink, whether or not you smoke and how much sleep you get — will all have a knock-on effect on your fitness and your health.

2) If you have a sedentary lifestyle, it means you don't exercise enough:

> A SEDENTARY LIFESTYLE is one where there is irregular or no physical activity.

3) If you aren't active enough, you don't use up all the energy you get from food. Any excess energy is stored as fat, which increases your risk of becoming overweight or obese (see below).

A **Sedentary Lifestyle** has Many **Long-term Health Risks**

A SEDENTARY LIFESTYLE CAN CAUSE:

- Lethargy (always feeling tired).
- Poor sleep.
- Emotional health problems like low confidence and self-esteem, poor body image and depression.
- Poor social health — it becomes hard to leave the home and socialise with others.
- Obesity (having a large amount of body fat).

1) Obesity puts more strain on your cardiovascular system and decreases cardiovascular endurance.

2) Increased body fat can also lead to high cholesterol and fatty deposits in the arteries, making it harder for the heart to pump blood. This can lead to hypertension (high blood pressure) and the risk of strokes and coronary heart disease.

3) You are also more likely to develop type-2 diabetes (see p.89) if you are obese, and are more at risk of getting certain cancers.

4) Being overweight decreases flexibility, speed, power and agility, so affects your performance too.

> Even if you're a healthy weight, being inactive will still put you at risk of health problems.

You can use **BMI** to Determine if Someone is **Obese**

1) Your Body Mass Index (BMI) score is calculated using your height and weight. Your score is used to classify you as underweight, of healthy weight, overweight or obese. The thresholds used depend on a person's ethnicity:

> People in black, Asian or certain other minority ethnic groups are at a higher risk of obesity-related health problems at a lower BMI.

	UNDERWEIGHT	HEALTHY WEIGHT	OVERWEIGHT	OBESE
People of white heritage	BMI of below 18.5	BMI between 18.5 and 25	BMI of 25 or over	BMI of 30 or over
People in black, Asian or certain other minority ethnic groups	BMI of below 18.5	BMI between 18.5 and 23	BMI of 23 or over	BMI of 27.5 or over

2) BMI doesn't take into account muscle mass or bone structure, so it can incorrectly classify healthy, muscular people as overweight or obese.

A sedentary lifestyle can cause serious health problems...

It is important to avoid a sedentary lifestyle by staying active. Make sure you learn all the definitions and health risks on this page, then hop on over to the next page for some questions...

Warm-Up and Worked Exam Questions

There's a lot of stuff squeezed onto those three pages, so here are some questions to check that it's all sunk in. If there are questions here you struggle with, go back and read that page again.

Warm-Up Questions

1) What long-term effect can regular exercise have on blood pressure?
2) How does regular exercise help the musculo-skeletal system?
3) What is serotonin? How does it benefit an individual?
4) Explain how exercise can lead to an increase in someone's self-esteem.
5) Give one physical health risk of a sedentary lifestyle.
6) Give one way that being overweight could affect performance in tennis.
7) What weight classification is someone with a BMI of 35?

Worked Exam Questions

1   Khalid has just started a new job and is finding that he is feeling more stressed than he used to. A friend suggests that doing regular exercise may help.

(a) Explain how regular exercise could help Khalid. (Grade 3-5)

Exercise could help take Khalid's mind off things he is worried about,
which could help to reduce his stress levels.

[2 marks]

(b) Outline **two** ways exercise could help Khalid's social well-being. (Grade 1-3)

1 *It could give him an opportunity to meet new people and*
make new friends.

2 *If he joins a team he will have the opportunity to practise*
teamwork and cooperation with others.

[2 marks]

2   Outline the ways in which regular exercise improves physical health and well-being. (Grade 5-7)

Exercise improves heart function by keeping your heart strong, arteries elastic and
removing cholesterol from artery walls. Exercise helps to prevent obesity as it uses up
energy so your body doesn't have to store it as fat. Exercise helps to reduce the risk of
certain health problems, such as diabetes, by helping you to maintain a healthy weight.

[3 marks]

Exam Questions

1   Which **one** of these is a mental health benefit of exercise? (Grade 1-3)

Shade **one** oval only.

A   Regular exercise makes you stronger and more flexible   ⬭

B   Regular exercise helps you maintain a healthy weight   ⬭

C   Regular exercise improves your cardiovascular system   ⬭

D   Regular exercise can help you to reduce stress and tension   ⬭

[1 mark]

2   A sedentary lifestyle can lead to a wide range of health problems.

(a) Define a sedentary lifestyle. (Grade 1-3)

....

....

[1 mark]

(b) State **three** consequences of a sedentary lifestyle. (Grade 3-5)

1   ....

2   ....

3   ....

[3 marks]

3   Explain how exercise could benefit an individual with a manual labour job, such as a construction worker. (Grade 5-7)

> Think of the physical health benefits of exercise and how these could relate to a person with a manual labour job.

....

....

....

....

....

[2 marks]

Diet and Nutrition

To stay healthy you need a **balanced diet** — this means getting the **right amount** of **nutrients** for your **lifestyle**.

You Should Eat a **Balanced Diet** to be **Healthy**

1) Eating a balanced diet is an <u>important</u> part of being healthy and helps you perform well in sport.

2) What makes up a balanced diet is slightly <u>different</u> for everyone, depending on how <u>active</u> you are.

A balanced diet contains the <u>best ratio</u> of nutrients to match your lifestyle.

3) The '<u>best ratio</u>' means the <u>right amount</u> of each nutrient <u>in relation</u> to the other nutrients. There <u>isn't</u> one type of '<u>superfood</u>' that has <u>everything</u> your body needs — you need a <u>mix</u> of <u>foods</u>.

4) A balanced diet <u>supports</u> your lifestyle by providing the <u>nutrients</u> your body needs for <u>energy</u>, <u>growth</u> and <u>hydration</u>. It helps prevent <u>health problems</u> and <u>injury</u>, and to speed up <u>recovery</u> following exercise.

5) Your body needs large amounts of <u>carbohydrates</u>, <u>fats</u> and <u>proteins</u>. This pie chart shows the <u>rough amounts</u> of each that an average person should eat as part of a <u>balanced diet</u>:

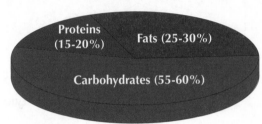

Proteins (15-20%) | Fats (25-30%) | Carbohydrates (55-60%)

CARBOHYDRATES

- For most people, carbohydrates are the main source of <u>energy</u> for the body. Carbohydrates are vital for providing energy for your <u>muscles</u> during <u>physical activity</u>.
- You can get <u>simple</u> ones like sugar, and <u>complex</u> ones, e.g. starch from pasta or rice.
- Whenever you eat carbohydrates, some will get <u>used</u> by the body <u>straight away</u>.
- The rest gets <u>stored</u> in the liver and muscles, ready for when it's needed (or turned into <u>fat</u>).

FATS

- Fats are made from molecules called <u>fatty acids</u>.
- They provide <u>more</u> energy than carbohydrates for <u>low-intensity</u> exercise. They also help to keep the <u>body warm</u> and <u>protect organs</u>, which helps to prevent injury.
- Some <u>vitamins</u> can <u>only</u> be absorbed by the body using fats.
- Too many <u>saturated fats</u> can cause <u>obesity</u>.

PROTEINS

- Proteins help the body <u>grow</u> and <u>repair itself</u>. They're vital for building and repairing <u>muscles</u> after <u>exercise</u>.
- They're made from molecules called <u>amino acids</u> — your body can make new proteins from the amino acids in food.
- <u>Meat</u>, <u>fish</u>, <u>eggs</u> and <u>beans</u> are all rich in protein.

Your **Energy Intake** and **Usage** Controls Your **Weight**

1) Energy from food is measured in <u>calories</u> (Kcal). On average, an adult <u>male</u> needs <u>2500 calories</u> a day, and an adult <u>female</u> needs <u>2000 calories</u> a day.

2) How much energy you need also depends on how much you use up through <u>bodily processes</u> (like breathing and digestion), <u>daily activities</u> and <u>exercise</u>. <u>Age</u> and <u>height</u> affect this too.

- If you take in <u>more</u> energy than you <u>use</u>, the <u>spare</u> energy is stored as <u>fat</u>, which causes you to <u>gain weight</u>.
- If you <u>don't</u> take in <u>enough</u> food to match the energy you need, your body <u>makes up the difference</u> by using up the energy stored in <u>body fat</u> and you <u>lose weight</u>.
- If you want to <u>maintain</u> a healthy weight, you need to make sure the energy you take in <u>matches</u> the energy you use up.

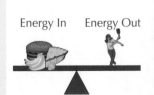

Energy In   Energy Out

A balanced diet is a key part of being healthy...

Make sure that you understand how carbohydrates, proteins and fats help you to do physical activity.

Diet and Nutrition

Good nutrition isn't just about eating the right amounts of carbohydrates, fats and proteins. **Vitamins** and **minerals** are important for **maintaining** body systems and general **health**, as is drinking plenty of **water**.

You need Small Amounts of Vitamins and Minerals

VITAMINS

1) Vitamins help your bones, teeth, skin and other tissues to grow. They're also needed for many of the body's chemical reactions, e.g. some are used in the processes that release energy from food.

2) Fat-soluble vitamins can be stored in the body. Here are a couple of examples:
   - Vitamin A — needed for your growth and vision.
   - Vitamin D — needed for strong bones so helps to prevent injury.

3) Water-soluble vitamins can't be stored, so you need to eat them regularly. For example:
   - Vitamin C — good for your skin and helps to hold your body tissues together. It's also really important for your immune system, so helps you to stay healthy so you can train and perform well.

MINERALS

1) Needed for healthy bones and teeth, and to build other tissues.

2) Minerals help in various chemical reactions in the body:
   - Calcium — needed for strong bones and teeth, but also for muscle contraction.
   - Iron — used in making red blood cells, which carry oxygen round the body, e.g. to the muscles.

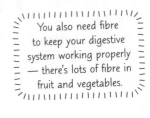

You also need fibre to keep your digestive system working properly — there's lots of fibre in fruit and vegetables.

Water is also Important for Good Health

WATER

1) Water is needed in loads of chemical reactions in the body. It's also used in sweat to help you cool down when your body temperature rises, e.g. through exercise. As well as sweating, you also lose water through your breath, urine and faeces.

2) If you don't drink enough to replace the water you've used or lost, you become dehydrated. This means your body doesn't have enough water to work well — it's not hydrated, which can cause:
   - Blood thickening — you guessed it, the blood gets thicker (more viscous). This makes it harder for the heart to pump the blood around — it has to work harder and beat faster. It also decreases the flow of oxygen to the muscles, so you can't perform as well in aerobic exercise, e.g. swimming.
   - Slower reactions and poor decision-making, as your brain needs water to function well. A boxer is less likely to be able to dodge an incoming punch.
   - An increase in body temperature, as without enough water the body can't sweat effectively. This can cause overheating and maybe even fainting through heat exhaustion.
   - Muscle fatigue and cramps, which could mean you have to stop doing an activity. Endurance athletes — like marathon runners — may not be able to finish their event.

3) Rehydration with water or sports drinks during and after physical activity helps avoid dehydration. This is important in endurance events and hot climates where you sweat more.

4) Sports drinks have sugar in them to replace the energy your muscles have used up. They also contain a bit of salt which helps the water rehydrate you quickly.

Diet isn't just what you eat — staying hydrated is important too...

Make sure that you understand how being dehydrated can have a negative effect on performance.

Somatotypes

Somatotype means the basic **shape** of your **body**. Your somatotype can affect your **suitability** for a particular sport. Learn the somatotypes and make sure you can **identify** which type suits what sport.

Somatotypes are Body Types

There are three <u>basic</u> somatotypes — <u>ectomorph</u>, <u>mesomorph</u> and <u>endomorph</u>.
Very few people are a perfect example of one of these body types — pretty much everyone is a <u>mixture</u>.
You can think of these basic somatotypes as <u>extremes</u> — at the corners of a triangular graph.

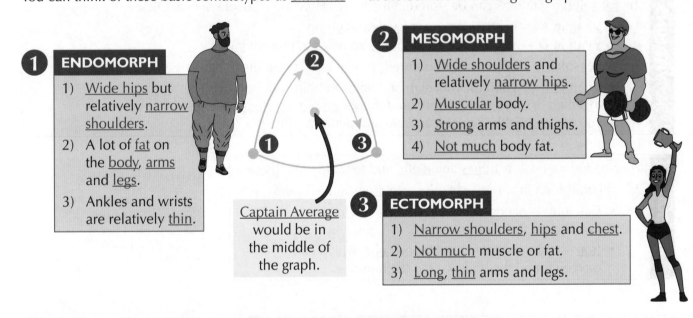

1 ENDOMORPH
1) <u>Wide hips</u> but relatively <u>narrow shoulders</u>.
2) A lot of <u>fat</u> on the <u>body</u>, <u>arms</u> and <u>legs</u>.
3) Ankles and wrists are relatively <u>thin</u>.

2 MESOMORPH
1) <u>Wide shoulders</u> and relatively <u>narrow hips</u>.
2) <u>Muscular</u> body.
3) <u>Strong</u> arms and thighs.
4) <u>Not much</u> body fat.

3 ECTOMORPH
1) <u>Narrow shoulders</u>, <u>hips</u> and <u>chest</u>.
2) <u>Not much</u> muscle or fat.
3) <u>Long</u>, <u>thin</u> arms and legs.

<u>Captain Average</u> would be in the middle of the graph.

Different Somatotypes suit Different Sports

Certain body types are <u>better suited</u> for certain sports — the right body type can give you an <u>advantage</u>.

<u>Endomorphs</u> are usually best at activities like <u>wrestling</u> and <u>shot-put</u> — where <u>weight</u> and a <u>low centre of mass</u> (see p.35) can be an advantage.

E.g. in sumo wrestling, being <u>heavy</u> and having a <u>low centre of mass</u> makes it much harder for your opponent to <u>throw</u> you around the wrestling ring.

<u>Ectomorphs</u> suit activities like the <u>high jump</u> and <u>long-distance running</u> — where being <u>light</u> and having <u>long legs</u> is an advantage. They <u>don't</u> usually suit activities where <u>strength</u> is important.

E.g. high jumpers need to be <u>light</u> so they have <u>less weight</u> to lift over the bar. The taller the jumper, the <u>shorter</u> the distance they (and their centre of mass) have to travel to be able to get over the bar.

<u>Mesomorphs</u> are suited to <u>most types</u> of activity:
1) They're able to build up <u>muscle</u> relatively quickly and easily — which gives them an advantage in any activity where <u>strength</u> is important. E.g. sprinting, tennis, weightlifting...
2) Mesomorphs also have <u>broad shoulders</u>, which make it easier for them to be able to <u>support</u> weight using their upper body. This can be a huge advantage in activities like <u>weightlifting</u> and <u>gymnastics</u>.

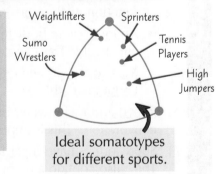

Ideal somatotypes for different sports.

Here's a bunch of long words for you to learn...

To remember which somatotype is which, just think that a **M**esomorph is **M**uscular and an ec**T**omorph is **T**hin. So, the one that isn't muscular or thin must be an endomorph.

Warm-Up and Worked Exam Questions

There are a lot of facts on the last few pages, so make sure you've got them all with the warm-up and worked exam questions below, and the exam questions on the next page.

Warm-Up Questions

1) What percentage of an average person's balanced diet should be made up of carbohydrates?
2) What unit is energy from food measured in?
3) List three factors which determine a person's energy requirement.
4) Give one reason why the body needs minerals.
5) Give two consequences of dehydration.
6) Which somatotype has narrow shoulders, hips and chest?
7) Name a sport that an endomorph is well-suited to play.

Worked Exam Questions

1   Complete **Table 1** below describing the roles of different nutrients. Grade 1-3

Nutrient	Role in a balanced diet
Vitamins and minerals	_Maintaining healthy body systems._
Proteins	Repairing muscle
Carbohydrates	_Energy for all intensities of exercise._

Table 1

[3 marks]

2   Simone is playing a tennis match. Grade 5-7

Evaluate the consequences of dehydration for Simone.

Dehydration could cause Simone to have slower reaction times, so she might not be able to return serves as effectively. She might get muscle fatigue and cramps and be unable to run to the ball, and her body temperature might increase so that she becomes faint and is unable to finish the match.

[3 marks]

There are other consequences you can mention here — you need to explain how at least three effects of dehydration may affect her performance in the match to get all the marks.

Exam Questions

1 Which **one** of these is the recommended balance of carbohydrates, fats and proteins in the diet of an average person? **Grade 1-3**

Shade **one** oval only.

A 50-55% carbohydrates, 35-40% fats, 10-15% proteins ⬭

B 55-60% carbohydrates, 25-30% fats, 15-20% proteins ⬭

C 55-60% carbohydrates, 35-40% fats, 5-10% proteins ⬭

D 40-45% carbohydrates, 25-30% fats, 30-25% proteins ⬭

[1 mark]

2 Abby has a muscular body, wide shoulders and not much body fat.

(a) Suggest which somatotype Abby might be. **Grade 3-5**

....

[1 mark]

(b) State **one** sport that Abby would be suited to. Justify your answer. **Grade 5-7**

....

....

....

[2 marks]

3 Outline the role of carbohydrates and fats in physical activity and evaluate their importance for a marathon runner.

....

....

....

....

....

....

....

....

....

....

[6 marks]

Revision Summary

Knowledge Organiser Quick Quiz

It's time to check your Health, Fitness and Well-being ~~status~~ knowledge. You can:
- Use the **Knowledge Organiser** to go over all the **key points**.
- Try an **online quiz** for a quick bit of **extra practice**.
- Tackle the **summary questions** below. Yes, they're hard — try to answer them **from memory** to **really test** how well you know the topic. The **answers** are all **in the section**, so go over anything **you're unsure of** again.

Health, Fitness and Well-being (p.89-90) ☑

1) How does physical activity affect your: a) cardiovascular system? b) weight?

2) Regular physical exercise improves your musculo-skeletal system.
Explain how this can reduce your chances of getting injured during physical activity.

3) Name two long-term health conditions that regular exercise can help you avoid.
How does exercise reduce your risk of getting them?

4) Give four emotional benefits that exercise can have.

5) What is social health and well-being? How can taking part in physical activity improve your social health and well-being?

Sedentary Lifestyle (p.91) ☑

6) What is a 'sedentary lifestyle'? How is it connected to obesity?

7) Give five negative impacts that a sedentary lifestyle can have on your health and well-being.

8) What are four long-term health risks associated with obesity?

9) How might obesity affect performance in physical activity and sport?

10) Name the two factors that are needed to calculate Body Mass Index (BMI).

11) What weight classification is someone with a BMI score of 26?
Why might this be misleading?

Diet and Nutrition (p.94-95) ☑

12) What is a 'balanced diet'? Why should you eat a balanced diet?

13) A balanced diet should contain roughly what percentage of: a) carbohydrates? b) proteins? c) fats?

14) Name the nutrient that is the main source of energy for most people during physical activity.

15) Why do you need fat in your diet?

16) How does protein help you to recover after exercise?

17) How many calories a day are required by: a) an average adult male? b) an average adult female?
Which other factors affect how much energy you need?

18) What happens to your weight if you take in more energy than you use?

19) Give two reasons why the body needs vitamins. What does the body use minerals for?

20) What is dehydration?

21) Explain what happens to your blood when you become dehydrated.

22) Give three other effects of dehydration on the body.

Somatotypes (p.96) ☑

23) What are the main characteristics of: a) an endomorph? b) a mesomorph? c) an ectomorph?

24) Describe the types of sports that endomorphs are suited to.

25) What sorts of sports might mesomorphs be good at?

26) Explain why an ectomorph would be well suited to long-distance running.

Using Data

You've got to be comfortable with **interpreting data** displayed in **graphs** and **tables**. Luckily for you, these **four pages** will go through **how** you do it. And you thought you could get **away** from maths by taking PE...

There Are **Two** Different **Types** of **Data**

You can collect <u>two</u> different types of <u>data</u> — <u>qualitative</u> data and <u>quantitative</u> data:

<u>Qualitative data <u>describes</u> something — it will be in <u>words</u>.

1) Qualitative data can be collected through <u>observation</u> — e.g. 'the team <u>played well</u>', 'the athlete is <u>strong</u>' or 'the weather was <u>cold</u>'.

2) Or you can <u>interview</u> people. E.g. asking an athlete how they're <u>feeling</u> before a race might give you answers like "<u>confident</u>" or "<u>well-prepared</u>".

3) It's less easy to <u>analyse</u> than data in numbers.

<u>Quantitative data <u>measures</u> something — it will be in <u>numbers</u>.

1) Quantitative data <u>measures</u> things — e.g. '<u>time taken</u> to finish a race' or '<u>weight</u> of an athlete'.

2) All the <u>fitness tests</u> (see pages 37-40) give quantitative data, as the results are <u>numbers</u>. You can also use <u>surveys</u> or <u>questionnaires</u> to collect <u>quantitative</u> data.

3) Quantitative data can be represented in <u>tables</u> and <u>graphs</u>, so it's easier to <u>analyse</u>.

You need to be able to **Plot** a **Bar Chart** from a **Table**

In the exam you might be asked to <u>plot</u> a <u>bar chart</u> using a <u>table</u> of data. You might know how to do this already, but it <u>never hurts</u> to go over it <u>again</u>. Below is a <u>bar chart</u> for the following data on <u>BMI</u>:

Number of students with each Body Mass Index (BMI) category

BMI category	Underweight	Healthy Weight	Overweight	Obese
No. of students	45	151	115	39

A scale for the <u>values</u> goes on the <u>y-axis</u> (up the side).

Leave a <u>gap</u> between <u>each bar</u>.

- The <u>height</u> of each bar shows the <u>data value</u> for that category — the <u>taller</u> the <u>bar</u>, the <u>bigger</u> the <u>value</u>.
- <u>Plotting</u> data as a <u>bar chart</u> makes it easy to <u>compare</u> categories. It's really <u>easy</u> to see the <u>largest</u> and <u>smallest</u> values.

The different <u>categories</u> go on the <u>x-axis</u> (along the bottom).

You get one mark just for <u>labelling the axes</u> — so don't forget...

No. of Students / BMI Category (Underweight, Healthy weight, Overweight, Obese)

Quantitative is numbers — qualitative is words...

It's easy to mix up 'qualitative' and 'quantitative', so check you're using the right word. The best way to remember the difference is 'quantitative' sounds like 'quantity', which means 'number of'.

Using Data

This page is all about **line graphs** — you need to know how to **plot** them and how to **analyse** them.

You can **Plot** a **Line Graph** from a **Table**

In the exam, you might be asked to plot a line graph from a table. You might know how to do this already, but it never hurts to go over it again... I seem to be having déjà vu.

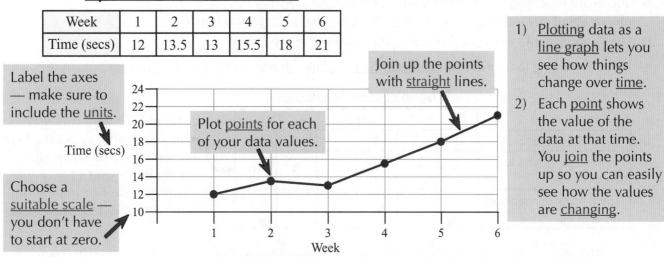

Riyad's results for the stork stand test

Week	1	2	3	4	5	6
Time (secs)	12	13.5	13	15.5	18	21

Label the axes — make sure to include the units.

Choose a suitable scale — you don't have to start at zero.

Plot points for each of your data values.

Join up the points with straight lines.

1) Plotting data as a line graph lets you see how things change over time.

2) Each point shows the value of the data at that time. You join the points up so you can easily see how the values are changing.

You can **Analyse** a **Line Graph**

To analyse a line graph you pick out certain bits of information and describe what's happening. You can:

IDENTIFY A SPECIFIC POINT — e.g. the highest/lowest value or the value at a particular time.
COMPARE DATA — from two sets of data (e.g. 'males' and 'females') or two times.
SPOT PATTERNS — whether the data is generally increasing, decreasing or staying the same.

Here's an example that shows how two sets of data (for two rugby players) can be analysed.

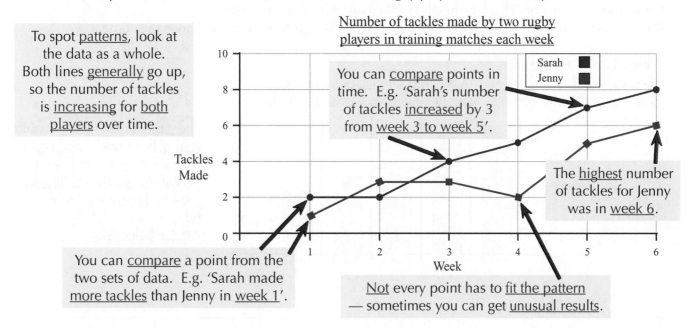

Number of tackles made by two rugby players in training matches each week

To spot patterns, look at the data as a whole. Both lines generally go up, so the number of tackles is increasing for both players over time.

You can compare points in time. E.g. 'Sarah's number of tackles increased by 3 from week 3 to week 5'.

The highest number of tackles for Jenny was in week 6.

You can compare a point from the two sets of data. E.g. 'Sarah made more tackles than Jenny in week 1'.

Not every point has to fit the pattern — sometimes you can get unusual results.

Revision patterns — amount of knowledge is increasing over time...

If you can analyse graphs and spot patterns, you'll breeze through any graph questions in the exam.

Using Data

You can analyse **physical fitness** by looking at **data** — on this page, you'll see how **tables** and **bar charts** can be used to analyse a person's fitness.

You can **Analyse** your **Fitness** over **Time**

1) You can measure <u>components of fitness</u> by doing regular <u>fitness tests</u>, and <u>comparing</u> the data you get <u>over time</u>.

2) You might have to <u>describe</u> what the data shows and say what this means about any <u>training</u> — i.e. if it's <u>working</u> or what <u>changes</u> are needed.

3) Here's an example of the kind of thing you might see in the exam:

Bryan is training to improve his <u>cardiovascular endurance</u> and his <u>maximal strength</u>.

Bryan's Fitness Test Results

Fitness Test	Week					
	1	2	3	4	5	6
Multi-stage fitness test score (level)	7	7	8	9	9	10
Bench press one rep max (mass in kg)	65	66	65	66	64	65

The MSFT data shows that Bryan is gradually getting <u>better</u> at the test — he completes more levels <u>over time</u>. This suggests he's improving his <u>cardiovascular endurance</u>.

The one rep max data shows that the heaviest weight Bryan can bench press is <u>staying about the same</u> (approximately 65 kg). This suggests that his <u>maximal strength</u> is fairly <u>constant</u>.

For more on fitness testing see Section Three.

Another way to <u>interpret</u> your scores in fitness tests is to <u>compare</u> them to <u>national averages</u> or <u>ratings tables</u> for your <u>age group</u> or <u>sex</u>. For an example of this, see page 40.

Bar Charts can show Fitness Data

Remember that on a bar chart the <u>heights</u> of the <u>bars</u> show the <u>data values</u>. This means you can spot <u>patterns</u> by looking at how the <u>heights of the bars</u> change over <u>time</u>.

Week 1 has the <u>tallest</u> bar, so Bryan's <u>resting heart rate</u> was <u>highest</u> in week 1.

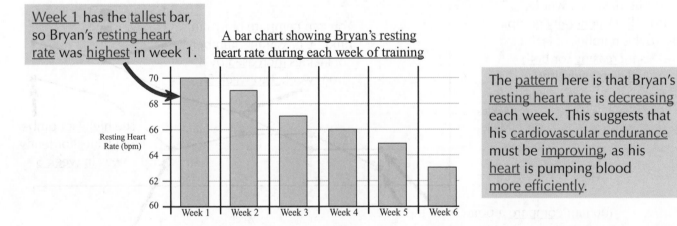

A bar chart showing Bryan's resting heart rate during each week of training

The <u>pattern</u> here is that Bryan's <u>resting heart rate</u> is <u>decreasing</u> each week. This suggests that his <u>cardiovascular endurance</u> must be <u>improving</u>, as his <u>heart</u> is pumping blood <u>more efficiently</u>.

The key to understanding fitness tests is understanding data...

Make sure you're comfortable analysing data about fitness — the data could be shown in a table, bar chart, line graph or pie chart. Have another look over pages 37 to 40 to check you know all the fitness tests.

Using Data

More **data**? Well okay, go on then — I know how much you **love** it. This page is about delicious **pie charts** and other less delicious ways to **interpret data**. Needless to say, you have to **learn it all**.

Pie Charts Show Proportions

1) Pie charts are a good way to compare different categories — such as age groups or gender.

2) The amount of the whole chart a section takes up tells you the proportion in that category — the whole chart represents everybody.

3) It's important to remember that pie charts show proportions, not the actual number in each category.

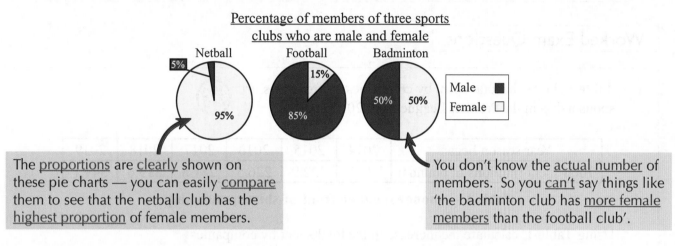

Percentage of members of three sports clubs who are male and female

Netball — 5%, 95%
Football — 15%, 85%
Badminton — 50%, 50%

Male ■
Female □

The proportions are clearly shown on these pie charts — you can easily compare them to see that the netball club has the highest proportion of female members.

You don't know the actual number of members. So you can't say things like 'the badminton club has more female members than the football club'.

4) You could be given one pie chart with lots of categories — e.g. a pie chart showing the proportion of money the government spends on different sports.

5) You don't need to be able to draw pie charts, just interpret them.

Interpret Data in the Context of the Question

To interpret data, you'll need to describe what it shows — you might also have to suggest possible reasons for the results using your PE knowledge.

EXAMPLE

The council of a large town carries out a survey to find out participation rates in football for different age groups. The bar chart below shows the results of the survey.

Interpret the bar chart and suggest one reason to explain the results.

E.g. The participation rate in football decreases as people get older.

There are lots of reasons that could explain the decrease in participation (see page 73), such as:

- The 11-20 category could be the highest because children might play football in PE at school.

- Older people may have other commitments — e.g. families, careers, etc.

- Football is a strenuous sport and older people could be physically limited.

- There might be a scheme that encourages younger people to play football.

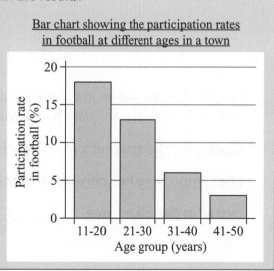

Bar chart showing the participation rates in football at different ages in a town

In the exam, any interpretation would get you the marks as long as it's suitable and you can justify it.

104

Warm-Up and Worked Exam Questions

Data could crop up in any PE topic, so it's important you get to grips with everything covered in this section. Go through the warm-up and worked exam questions carefully before you try the exam style questions.

Warm-Up Questions

1) Give two ways of collecting quantitative data.
2) If a line graph slopes upwards from left to right, what can you say about the data values?
3) What can fitness testing data tell you about your training?

Worked Exam Questions

1   **Table 1** shows the total spent by companies on front-of-shirt sponsorship in the Premier League from 2014 to 2019.

Year season began	2014	2015	2016	2017	2018	2019
Total spent (millions of pounds)	191.35	222.9	226.5	281.8	315.6	349.1

Table 1 — money spent on front-of-shirt sponsorship

Using **Table 1**, calculate the increase in the total spent by companies on front-of-shirt sponsorship in the Premier League from 2014 to 2019.

£349.1 million − £191.35 million = £157.75 million

[1 mark]

2   A GCSE student is training for a 5 km race. She does a multi-stage fitness test each week for four weeks. **Figure 1** shows the level that she scores each week.

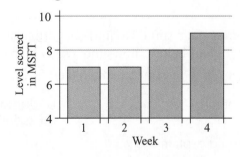

Figure 1 — MSFT results

Interpret the data shown in **Figure 1** and suggest how what it shows will affect the student's performance in the race.

Generally, the student's MSFT level is increasing over time. This suggests that she's improving her cardiovascular endurance, which means she should perform better in the 5 km race.

[3 marks]

Section Seven — Using Data

Exam Questions

1   **Figure 1** shows participation rates for three activities in England.

Graph showing the number of English people aged 16 or over who
participated at least twice in the previous 28 days, between 2016 and 2022.

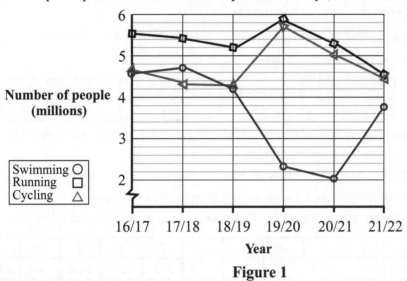

Figure 1

Analyse the data in **Figure 1**.

(a) State whether **Figure 1** shows qualitative or quantitative data. (Grade 3-5)
     Explain your answer.

     ....

     ....

     [2 marks]

(b) Suggest what is most likely to happen to the participation rate in running in 22/23. (Grade 5-7)
     Use **Figure 1** to justify your answer.

     ....

     ....

     ....

     [2 marks]

(c) Identify the activity in **Figure 1** that saw the greatest decrease in participation
     from 16/17 to 17/18 and suggest **one** reason to explain these results. (Grade 5-7)

     ....

     ....

     ....

     ....

     [3 marks]

Revision Summary

Well, that's the data all plotted — time to analyse your skills in Using Data. Tackle the **summary questions** below. Yes, they're hard — try to answer them **from memory** to **really test** how well you know the topic. The **answers** and **skills** you need are all **in the section**, so go over anything **you're unsure of** again.

Using Data (p.100-103)

1) What is the difference between quantitative and qualitative data?

2) Give two ways of collecting qualitative data and two ways of collecting quantitative data.

3) Do fitness tests give qualitative or quantitative data?

4) Look at this table of data:

BMI category	Underweight	Healthy Weight	Overweight	Obese
No. of students	45	151	115	39

   a) If you were plotting a bar chart from this data, what would go on the x-axis? How about the y-axis?

   b) Which BMI category contains the smallest number of students?
      How would this bar compare to the other bars on the bar chart?

5) A cyclist records their average speed over 12 weeks of training in the table below.
Plot a line graph to represent the data in the table. Don't forget to give it a title and label your axes.

Week	1	2	3	4	5	6	7	8	9	10	11	12
Average speed (km/h)	21.0	21.2	21.8	22.2	22.0	22.2	23.0	22.6	24.0	24.4	24.8	25.0

6) Give three ways that you can analyse a line graph to describe what it is showing.

7) Look at this line graph:

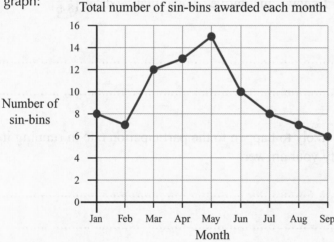

Total number of sin-bins awarded each month

   a) How many sin-bins were awarded in March? How many more were awarded in May?

   b) What pattern does the data show from May to September?

8) Give two ways you could analyse data from fitness tests in order to draw conclusions from the results.

9) Look at these pie charts:

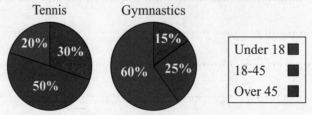

Percentage of players of different ages for two sports at a sports centre

   a) Which sport has a higher proportion of players aged 18-45?

   b) Can you tell from these pie charts which sport has a higher number of players aged over 45?
      Why or why not?

Practice Papers

Once you've been through all the questions in this book, you should be starting to feel prepared for the final exams. As a last bit of preparation, here are two practice exam papers for you to try. Paper 1 will test you on the topics in Sections 1-3 and 7 of this book, and Paper 2 will test you on the topics in Sections 4-7.

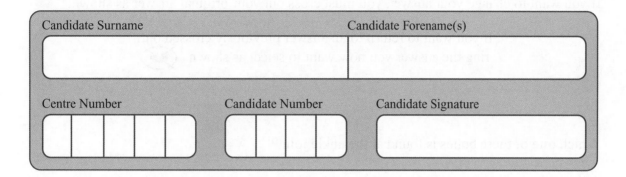

GCSE

Physical Education

Paper 1: The human body and movement
in physical activity and sport

Practice Paper
Time allowed: 1 hour 15 minutes

You are **allowed** to use a calculator.

Instructions to candidates

- Use **black** ink to write your answers.
- Write your name and other details in the spaces provided above.
- Answer **all** questions in the spaces provided.
- In calculations show clearly how you worked out your answers.

Information for candidates

- The marks available are given in brackets at the end of each question.
- There are 78 marks available for this paper.

Advice

- Carefully read each question before answering it.
- Try to answer every question.
- Write your answers clearly, using good English and the correct PE vocabulary.
- If you have time after finishing the paper, go back and check your answers.

Answer **ALL** the questions.

For questions with four responses, only **one** answer is allowed.

For each question you should shade in the oval alongside your answer as shown. ⬤

If you want to change your answer, you must cross out your original answer as shown. ✖

If you want to return to an answer previously crossed out,
ring the answer you now want to select as shown. ⊗

1   Which **one** of these bones is found at the ankle joint?

    A   Scapula   ◯

    B   Ulna   ◯

    C   Tibia   ◯

    D   Femur   ◯

[1 mark]

2   Which **one** of these muscles is responsible for extension at the elbow?

    A   Biceps   ◯

    B   Triceps   ◯

    C   Hip flexors   ◯

    D   Gluteals   ◯

[1 mark]

3   Which **one** of these describes a third class lever system?

    A   The load is between the fulcrum and effort   ◯

    B   The fulcrum is between the effort and load   ◯

    C   The effort is at the end of the lever   ◯

    D   The effort is between the fulcrum and load   ◯

[1 mark]

4   Identify the type of movement that would occur in the sagittal plane.

    A   Flexion   ◯

    B   Abduction   ◯

    C   Rotation   ◯

    D   Adduction   ◯

[1 mark]

5   Which **one** of these components of fitness is most important for a marathon runner?

    A   Reaction time   ◯

    B   Cardiovascular endurance   ◯

    C   Speed   ◯

    D   Muscular strength   ◯

[1 mark]

6   Which **one** of these training methods can be used to improve both aerobic and anaerobic fitness?

    A   Continuous training   ◯

    B   Weight training   ◯

    C   Plyometric training   ◯

    D   Circuit training   ◯

[1 mark]

7   Which **one** of these is a correct statement about alveoli?

    A   Alveoli have a small surface area   ◯

    B   Alveoli have thick, muscular walls   ◯

    C   Alveoli have access to a large blood supply   ◯

    D   Alveoli remove oxygen from red blood cells   ◯

[1 mark]

8   Tendons are part of the musculo-skeletal system.

Outline the role of tendons in movement of the skeleton.

....

....

....

....

[2 marks]

9   The cardiovascular system undergoes many changes during exercise.

9.1   Outline how blood is redistributed around the body during exercise.

....

....

....

....

[2 marks]

9.2   State **two** other immediate effects of exercise on the cardiovascular system.

1 ....

....

2 ....

....

[2 marks]

10   **Figure 1** shows a diver standing on their toes in preparation for a dive.

Figure 1

10.1 Draw the lever system operating in **Figure 1** and label the fulcrum, effort and load.

[1 mark]

10.2 Interpret the mechanical advantage of the lever in **Figure 1**.

....

....

....

....

[2 marks]

11   Using a sporting example of your choice, outline how **two** long-term effects
of regular exercise would benefit performers of that sport.

1 ....

....

2 ....

....

[2 marks]

12 **Figure 2** shows an athlete preparing to jump during plyometric training.
The jumping action uses different synovial joints, including the knee joint.

Figure 2

12.1 Describe **two** features of a synovial joint, such as the knee joint.

....

....

....

....
[2 marks]

12.2 Identify the type of movement that occurs at the knee joint as the athlete
moves from an upright position to the position shown in **Figure 2**.

....
[1 mark]

12.3 Explain how the antagonistic muscle pair at the knee joint enables the athlete to jump.

....

....

....

....

....

....
[3 marks]

13 Discuss the impact on performance of using anaerobic respiration during a swimming race.

....

....

....

....

....

....

....

....

[4 marks]

14 Colin is 40 years old.

14.1 Calculate his theoretical maximum heart rate.

....

[1 mark]

14.2 Calculate the upper and lower thresholds of his anaerobic target zone.

....

....

....

....

....

[4 marks]

15 The sit and reach test and the vertical jump test are two fitness tests.

15.1 Describe how to carry out the sit and reach test.

....

....

....

....

[2 marks]

15.2 The sit and reach test measures a performer's flexibility.
Explain how a high level of flexibility can improve a long jumper's performance.

....

....

....

....

....

....

[3 marks]

15.3 Describe how to carry out the vertical jump test.

....

....

....

....

[2 marks]

15.4 Discuss the importance of the vertical jump test for a beach volleyball player.

....

....

....

....

....

....

[3 marks]

16 There are different aims of each of the three training seasons in sport.

Using a sporting example of your choice, outline **two** benefits to a performer of taking part in competition (peak) training.

1 ....

....

....

2 ....

....

....

[2 marks]

17 Suggest and explain **two** actions that a rugby player can take to help them avoid injury while playing their sport.

1 ....

....

....

....

2 ....

....

....

....

[4 marks]

18 Progressive overload and specificity are two of the principles of training.

    18.1 Define the term progressive overload.

        ....

        ....

        [1 mark]

    18.2 Suggest **one** way of using progressive overload in a javelin thrower's training.

        ....

        ....

        ....

        [2 marks]

    18.3 Milly plays for her school hockey team.
           To improve her performance, Milly trains by jogging for half an hour twice a week.

           Discuss whether her training applies the training principle of specificity.

        ....

        ....

        ....

        ....

        ....

        ....

        [3 marks]

19   Jamal uses a heart rate monitor during a 50-minute training session with his running club. **Figure 3** shows his heart rate values during the session.

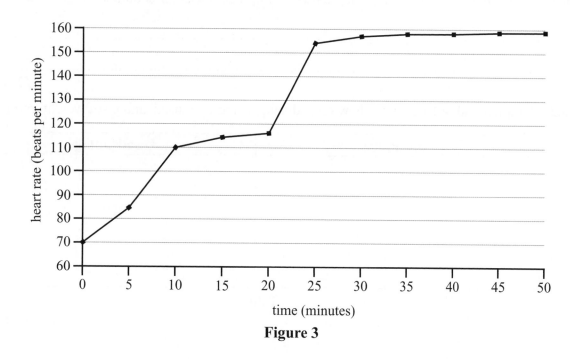

Figure 3

Using **Figure 3**, analyse Jamal's heart rate at the following times to suggest what may have happened in his training session during those times. Justify your answers.

*   Between 0 and 20 minutes
*   Between 20 and 50 minutes

....

....

....

....

....

....

[4 marks]

20   Weight training can be used to improve strength and muscular endurance.

20.1 Outline how weight training can be used to improve muscular endurance.

....

....

[2 marks]

20.2 Complete **Table 1** below to show **one** advantage and **one** disadvantage of weight training.

Advantage	Disadvantage

Table 1

[2 marks]

21   Using your knowledge of muscular endurance and agility, evaluate the importance of these components of fitness for performers in netball.

....

....

....

....

....

....

....

....

....

....

....

....

....

....

[6 marks]

22 Outline how the tidal volume of a midfielder changes during a football match and evaluate the importance of these changes for the performance of a midfielder.

....

....

....

....

....

....

....

....

....

....

....

....

....

....

....

....

....

....

....

....

....

....

....

....

....

....

[9 marks]

TOTAL FOR PAPER = 78 MARKS

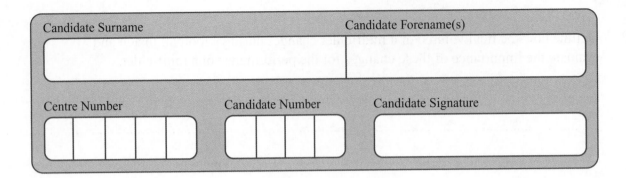

Candidate Surname		Candidate Forename(s)	
Centre Number	Candidate Number	Candidate Signature	

GCSE

Physical Education

Paper 2: Socio-cultural influences and well-being in physical activity and sport

Practice Paper
Time allowed: 1 hour 15 minutes

You are **allowed** to use a calculator.

Instructions to candidates
- Use **black** ink to write your answers.
- Write your name and other details in the spaces provided above.
- Answer **all** questions in the spaces provided.
- In calculations show clearly how you worked out your answers.

Information for candidates
- The marks available are given in brackets at the end of each question.
- There are 78 marks available for this paper.

Advice
- Carefully read each question before answering it.
- Try to answer every question.
- Write your answers clearly, using good English and the correct PE vocabulary.
- If you have time after finishing the paper, go back and check your answers.

Answer **ALL** the questions.

For questions with four responses, only **one** answer is allowed.

For each question you should shade in the oval alongside your answer as shown. ●

If you want to change your answer, you must cross out your original answer as shown. ✕

If you want to return to an answer previously crossed out,
ring the answer you now want to select as shown. ⊗

1   Which **one** of these is the proportion of carbohydrates required as part of a balanced diet?

A   25-30%   ○
B   35-40%   ○
C   45-50%   ○
D   55-60%   ○

[1 mark]

2   Which **one** of these is represented by the 'A' in 'SMART'?

A   Actual   ○
B   Accurate   ○
C   Accepted   ○
D   Accessible   ○

[1 mark]

3   Which **one** of these describes intrinsic feedback?

A   Feedback from how a performance feels to the performer   ○
B   Feedback that contains only positive comments   ○
C   Feedback from the audience at an event   ○
D   Feedback that a coach gives to a performer   ○

[1 mark]

4 Which **one** of these describes verbal guidance?

    A   When a learner uses sport equipment
          to help them learn a skill   ○

    B   When a coach physically moves a
          learner's body through a technique   ○

    C   When a learner watches someone else
          perform a technique before practising it   ○

    D   When a learner listens to an explanation
          of how to perform a technique   ○

[1 mark]

5 Which **one** of these is an example of gamesmanship?

    A   Time-wasting in football   ○

    B   Using performance-enhancing drugs   ○

    C   Deliberately tripping an opponent in football   ○

    D   Blood doping   ○

[1 mark]

6 Which **one** of these performers is most likely to use direct aggression?

    A   Rugby player   ○

    B   Golfer   ○

    C   Track cyclist   ○

    D   Rock climber   ○

[1 mark]

7   Exercise can improve physical, mental and social health and well-being.

    7.1   State **two** physical benefits of taking part in exercise.

        1 ....

        2 ....

                                    [2 marks]

    7.2   Outline **one** way that exercise can improve mental health.

        ....

        ....

        ....

                                      [2 marks]

    7.3   Exercise can help you to learn the skills of teamwork and cooperation. Identify whether this is a physical, mental or social benefit of exercise.

        ....

                                      [1 mark]

8   Maintaining water balance is essential to prevent dehydration.

    8.1   State **two** effects of dehydration.

        1 ....

        2 ....

                                      [2 marks]

    8.2   Using a sporting example of your choice, outline **one** way in which dehydration can affect the performers of that sport.

        ....

        ....

        ....

        ....

                                      [2 marks]

9 Studies have shown that people from some ethnic groups are more likely to participate in physical activity than others.

9.1 Explain **one** reason why an individual's ethnicity can affect their participation in sport.

....

....

....

[2 marks]

9.2 State **two** other personal factors, besides ethnicity or gender, that can affect an individual's participation in sport.

1 ....

2 ....

[2 marks]

10 A sedentary lifestyle is one factor that can contribute to obesity.

10.1 Define a sedentary lifestyle.

....

....

[1 mark]

10.2 Outline how an imbalance of energy intake and usage can cause obesity.

....

....

....

[2 marks]

10.3 Walter is obese. He wants to join a local swimming club. Explain **two** ways that obesity may affect his performance in swimming.

1 ....

....

....

....

2 ....

....

....

[4 marks]

11   Performers can become reliant on extrinsic motivation to continue participating in sport.

      Describe how extrinsic motivation can improve performance.
      Use an example in your answer.

      ....

      ....

      ....

      ....

                                                                                                    [2 marks]

12   A coach uses manual guidance when teaching a gymnast to perform a cartwheel on the beam.

      12.1 Complete **Table 1** below to show **one** advantage and
            one disadvantage of the coach using this guidance type.

Advantage	Disadvantage

                                        Table 1
                                                                                                    [2 marks]

      12.2 A gymnast may feel stressed if their routine involves complex skills.
            Outline **two** stress management techniques that a gymnast might use before a beam routine.

            1 ....

            ....

            ....

            2 ....

            ....

            ....

                                                                                                    [2 marks]

      12.3 Identify the somatotype that is most suited for gymnastics. Explain your choice.

            ....

            ....

            ....

                                                                                                    [2 marks]

13 Amanda sets herself a goal to complete an 80-mile bike ride in four months' time.

Analyse how the application of one of the principles of SMART in Amanda's goal will help her to achieve her goal.

....

....

....

....

....

....

[3 marks]

14 Spectators can have positive and negative effects at sporting events.

14.1 State **one** positive effect of spectators at a sporting event.

....

....

[1 mark]

14.2 One negative effect of spectators is the potential for hooliganism.
Suggest **two** reasons why hooliganism may occur at a football match.

1 ....

....

2 ....

....

[2 marks]

15 **Figure 1** shows the skill of catching by a wicket-keeper in cricket.

Figure 1

15.1 Define skill.

....

....

[1 mark]

15.2 Classify the skill shown in **Figure 1** into these skill classifications:

- gross or fine
- self-paced or externally-paced

Justify your answers.

....

....

....

....

[2 marks]

15.3 Describe how the stages of the information processing
model apply to the skill shown in **Figure 1**.

....

....

....

....

....

....

....

....

[4 marks]

16 Figures **2a** and **2b** show the number of people in England who participated in swimming and football at least twice in the previous 28 days between 2015 and 2022.

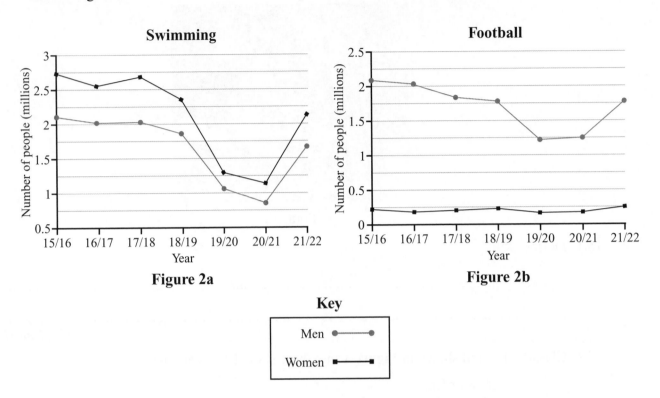

Figure 2a

Figure 2b

Key

Men ●——●

Women ■——■

Use **Figures 2a** and **2b** to describe the differences in participation levels between men and women in swimming and football, **and** suggest **one** reason for these differences in each sport.

....

....

....

....

....

....

....

....

[4 marks]

17   Some sportspeople display gamesmanship or use prohibited substances
      and methods to give themselves an advantage in competition.

      17.1 Define gamesmanship.

      ....Practice Paper 2

      ....
      [1 mark]

      17.2 Evaluate the impact of elite performers demonstrating
            gamesmanship in high profile sports, such as cricket.

      ....

      ....

      ....

      ....

      ....

      ....
      [3 marks]

      17.3 Describe what is meant by blood doping.

      ....

      ....

      ....

      ....
      [2 marks]

      17.4 Justify whether anabolic agents give the most significant performance
            benefit to a 100 m sprinter or an endurance athlete.

      ....

      ....

      ....

      ....

      ....
      [3 marks]

130

18 Sponsorship, sport and the media have grown to rely on one another.

Explain how financial sponsorship could have a positive effect on a sports team.

....

....

....

....

....

....

[3 marks]

19 With reference to different types of media, evaluate the impact
that increased media interest can have on sport.

....

....

....

....

....

....

....

....

....

....

....

....

....

[6 marks]

20 Outline what visual and mechanical guidance are and justify their use when coaching a group of beginners in trampolining.

....

....

....

....

....

....

....

....

....

....

....

....

....

....

....

....

....

....

....

....

....

....

....

....

....

....

[9 marks]

TOTAL FOR PAPER = 78 MARKS

Answers

<u>A note about marks and grades:</u>

The answers and mark schemes given here should be used mainly for guidance, as there may be many different correct answers to each question — don't panic if your answers are a bit different. The grade stamps are a rough guide to the level of difficulty of each question, and should not be used to predict the grade you'll get in the real exams.

Section One — Anatomy and Physiology

Page 10 (Warm-Up Questions)

1) Vital organs

2) E.g. The tibia. It is used when the lower leg flexes and extends to kick a football.

3) Flexion or dorsiflexion

4) E.g. The shoulder. It allows flexion, extension, adduction, abduction, rotation and circumduction.

5) Ligaments, tendons and cartilage

6) E.g. Synovial fluid lubricates joints to allow them to move more easily.

7) The gastrocnemius

8) Eccentric

9) Antagonistic muscle pair

10) Quadriceps and hamstrings

Page 11 (Exam Questions)

1 (a) Hinge joint *[1 mark]*

(b) Any **two** from: e.g.
- Ligaments hold the bones together to restrict movement.
- The joint capsule provides support.
- The synovial membrane releases synovial fluid.
- The synovial fluid lubricates the joint allowing it to move easily.
- Cartilage prevents friction between bones.
- Bones are shaped to fit together smoothly.
- Bursae reduce friction.
[1 mark for each up to a maximum of 2 marks]

2 E.g. The triceps are the agonist which contract to cause the movement from Position **A** to Position **B** *[1 mark]*. The triceps pull on the ulna and radius in the lower arm *[1 mark]*, causing extension at the elbow *[1 mark]*.

Page 16 (Warm-Up Questions)

1) Right atrium, right ventricle, left atrium and left ventricle

2) Diastole

3) Arteries

4) Red

5) Trachea

6) E.g. Residual volume is the volume of air left in the lungs, after you've breathed out as much air as you can.

Page 17 (Exam Questions)

1 **D** Alveoli *[1 mark]*

2 E.g. Arteries have thick, muscular walls *[1 mark]*, which allows them to carry blood flowing at high pressure *[1 mark]*.

3 (a) Tidal volume is the volume of air breathed in or out in one breath *[1 mark]*. Inspiratory reserve volume is the volume of air you can still breathe in after a normal breath *[1 mark]*.

(b) Tidal volume increases during exercise *[1 mark]*. Inspiratory reserve volume decreases during exercise *[1 mark]*.

4 E.g. Red blood cells carry oxygen *[1 mark]*, so a high number of red blood cells would lead to more oxygen being delivered to the muscles during exercise *[1 mark]*. This is very important for a marathon runner, as it would allow them to work aerobically for long periods *[1 mark]*.

Page 23 (Warm-Up Questions)

1) Aerobic

2) Carbon dioxide or water

3) Oxygen debt is the amount of oxygen needed to remove lactic acid and recover after doing anaerobic exercise.

4) Exercise causes an increase in breathing rate.

5) Stroke volume increases during exercise.

6) Cardiac output = heart rate × stroke volume

7) Any **one** from: e.g.
- Muscle hypertrophy
- Increased muscle strength
- Increased muscular endurance
- Stronger ligaments and tendons
- Increased suppleness

8) Cardiac hypertrophy is when the heart muscle gets bigger and stronger.

Pages 24-25 (Exam Questions)

1 **C** Delayed onset of muscle soreness *[1 mark]*
Increased heart rate and increase in tidal volume occur during / straight after exercise and change in body shape is a long-term effect.

2 (a)

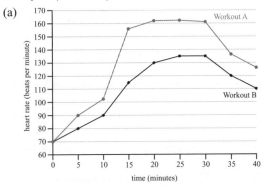

[1 mark for correctly plotted and joined up points]

(b) E.g. The performer's heart rate was much higher throughout workout A *[1 mark]*, which suggests that they exercised at a higher intensity than in workout B *[1 mark]*.

3 E.g. Swimming increases blood flow to the arm muscles *[1 mark]*. They would need more oxygenated blood *[1 mark]* in order to release the extra energy needed for swimming movements *[1 mark]*.
You could've identified leg muscles and/or said that the muscles would release more waste products, such as carbon dioxide or lactic acid, so they would need extra blood to remove them.

4 *This mark scheme gives examples of some points you might have made in your answer, and how many marks you would get for making those points. You can still get full marks if you haven't written every individual point below, as long as the points you have made are detailed enough.*

You will get up to two marks for showing knowledge and understanding of aerobic and anaerobic respiration, for example:

- Aerobic respiration uses glucose and oxygen to release energy.
- Aerobic respiration is needed for activities that require endurance.
- Anaerobic respiration uses glucose to release energy, but doesn't use oxygen.

You will get up to four marks if you also apply knowledge of aerobic and anaerobic respiration to a 50-mile cycling race, for example:

- Cycling for 50 miles would take several hours, so aerobic respiration would be needed for the majority of the race.
- Anaerobic respiration would be needed for high-intensity parts of the race, for example, when cycling on a steep gradient.
- Anaerobic respiration would be used for short bursts of speed on the bike, such as a sprint finish.

You will get up to nine marks if you also evaluate the importance of aerobic and anaerobic respiration for performance in a 50-mile cycling race, for example:

- A cyclist in a 50-mile race would want to mainly use aerobic respiration to ensure they can maintain a good performance throughout the race.
- A race is competitive and a cyclist using just aerobic exercise won't be able to cycle as quickly as other cyclists who can use anaerobic exercise to sprint more powerfully.
- Anaerobic respiration is important in a cycling race, because there will be parts of the race where short bursts of energy are needed, e.g. for a sprint finish.
- The cyclist may want to avoid cycling at speeds where anaerobic respiration is needed too often, as this would cause muscle fatigue, leading to a drop in performance.
- In conclusion, both types of respiration are important to achieve good overall performance in a 50-mile cycling race, as the performer must balance endurance with speed.
[9 marks available in total]

Section Two — Movement Analysis

Page 30 (Warm-Up Questions)

1) Muscles

2) E.g. At the ankle, when standing on the toes.

3) E.g.

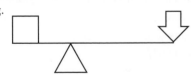

It doesn't matter if your diagram has the load and effort the opposite way around — as long as the fulcrum is closer to the load than it is to the effort.

4) Third class levers have a low mechanical advantage because the effort arm is always shorter than the weight arm.

5) The transverse plane divides the body into top and bottom.

6) Longitudinal

Page 31 (Exam Questions)

1 **D** Longitudinal *[1 mark]*

2 (a) Frontal plane *[1 mark]* and sagittal axis *[1 mark]*

(b) Sagittal plane *[1 mark]* and transverse axis *[1 mark]*

(c) Transverse plane *[1 mark]* and longitudinal axis *[1 mark]*

3 (a) Second class *[1 mark]*

(b) Second class levers have a high mechanical advantage, so can move large loads *[1 mark]* with a small effort from the muscles *[1 mark]*. This allows the gymnast to easily raise their entire body weight onto their toes *[1 mark]*.

Section Three — Physical Training

Page 41 (Warm-Up Questions)

1) E.g. Fitness is the ability to meet / cope with the demands of the environment.

2) E.g. Muscular endurance is the ability to repeatedly use muscles over a long time, without getting tired.

3) A gymnast holding a handstand.

4) Power is a combination of strength and speed.

5) Agility is more important for a squash player.

6) E.g. A gymnast needs good balance to keep themselves stable on the beam.

7) E.g. Reaction time is the time taken to move in response to a stimulus.

8) E.g. A high level of flexibility decreases the chances of pulling or straining muscles.

9) (a) Multi-stage fitness test

(b) Vertical jump test

(c) Wall toss test

10) E.g. Many of the tests do not test specific sporting actions. They do not tell you how an athlete will perform under pressure in a competition. Maximal tests can be inaccurate if the performer is not motivated and working at maximum effort. *You might have also said that fitness test scores can improve through practising them without the relevant components of fitness improving or that submaximal tests can be inaccurate.*

Pages 42-43 (Exam Questions)

1 **B** At the start of the race, when the starter pistol is fired *[1 mark]*

2 **A** Good *[1 mark]*

3 E.g. Power *[1 mark]*. More power will help Ben to throw the shot a further distance *[1 mark]*.

E.g. Balance *[1 mark]*. The action in shot-put involves rotating to generate power. Balance will help Ben to control this rotation, so his throwing action will be smooth and coordinated *[1 mark]*.
There are other answers you could give to this question as several components of fitness are involved in the shot-put. Just make sure your justification clearly shows how that component of fitness would help Ben improve his performance.

4 (a) Any **two** from: e.g.
- To identify strengths and weaknesses / fitness level before starting his training, so he can plan what to focus on.
- To monitor progress to see if his training is working or not.
- To compare his level of fitness to national averages.
- To set new goals or motivate himself.
- To provide variety in his training.
[1 mark for each up to a maximum of 2 marks]

(b) E.g. The Multi Stage Fitness Test measures cardiovascular endurance (aerobic power) *[1 mark]*, whereas the 30 m sprint test measures maximum sprint speed over a short distance *[1 mark]*. The triathlon is an endurance event that requires a high level of cardiovascular endurance, so the Multi Stage Fitness Test is more suitable for Eric *[1 mark]*.

(c) Eric's training is not improving his cardiovascular endurance *[1 mark]*.

5   *This mark scheme gives examples of some points you might have made in your answer, and how many marks you'd get for making those points. You can still get full marks if you haven't written every individual point below, as long as the points you've made are detailed enough.*

You will get one mark for showing knowledge and understanding of the sit and reach test and the Illinois agility test, for example:
- The sit and reach test measures the flexibility of the back and lower hamstrings.
- The Illinois agility test measures agility — whether you can change position or direction quickly, with control.

You will get up to three marks if you also apply knowledge of the sit and reach test and the Illinois agility test to a footballer, for example:
- Footballers need flexibility in their legs for a variety of skills.
- Footballers need agility to change direction during a match.

You will get up to six marks if you also evaluate the suitability of both tests for a footballer, for example:
- Footballers require flexible legs to make their running and their kicking actions smooth and efficient, so the sit and reach test is a useful test.
- The ability to quickly change direction and weave around opponents is one of the most important skills for a footballer.
- Footballers need agility to dribble past opponents and react to the position of the ball/other players — these skills are crucial to performance.
- However, these tests are not specific to football skills, e.g. technique for passing the ball.
- Other components of fitness, e.g. cardiovascular endurance, are also important and need to be tested.
[6 marks available in total]

Page 47 (Warm-Up Questions)

1) Overload is working the body harder than it would normally work.

2) E.g. Varying training is important as the same type of training can become boring and lead to a performer losing focus and motivation.

3) E.g. To give your muscles the chance to adapt, and to repair the damage caused by physical activity.

4) E.g. Your heart rate increases during exercise to increase the blood and oxygen supply to the working muscles.

5) $220 - 40 = 180$ (bpm)

6) Both

Page 48 (Exam Questions)

1   Fatima should spend more time training anaerobically *[1 mark]* as weightlifting requires short bursts of maximal effort, so is an anaerobic activity *[1 mark]*.

2   (a) E.g. Progressive overload means gradually increasing the amount of work you do in training to improve fitness *[1 mark]*. Lucy could do this by gradually increasing the distance she runs each week *[1 mark]*.

(b) Specificity means matching training to the activity and components of fitness you want to improve *[1 mark]*.

(c) E.g. Lucy could apply specificity to her training by making sure that most of her training involves running long distances without taking breaks *[1 mark]*.

3   $220 - 25 = 195$ *[1 mark]*.
195×0.8 *[1 mark]* = 156 bpm *[1 mark]*
You do 195×0.8 because the lower anaerobic threshold is 80% of maximum heart rate.

Page 55 (Warm-Up Questions)

1) Fartlek training is a type of continuous training that involves changing the intensity of the exercise over different intervals.

2) A rep is one single completed movement, whereas a set is a group of reps.

3) E.g. Weight training and plyometric training.

4) E.g. It takes a long time to set up.

5) E.g. Endurance athletes, because the increase in red blood cells helps them to perform aerobically for longer.

6) Pre-season (preparation) and post-season (transition).

7) E.g. Structured training means you avoid over training and can prevent overuse injuries. You can also match your fitness with the correct intensity to achieve overload.

8) Any **one** from: e.g.
- Leave enough recovery time
- Eat and rehydrate
- Complete a cool-down
- Take an ice bath
- Get a sports massage

9) Any **one** from: e.g.
- It prepares the muscles that are going to be used during an activity.
- It helps with mental preparation by focusing the performer on the activity and getting them "in the zone".

10) E.g. A cool down should involve gentle exercise to gradually reduce the intensity and stretching of the muscles that were used in the activity.

Pages 56-57 (Exam Questions)

1   Weight training can improve muscular endurance by using a low weight (below 70% of your one rep max) and a high number of reps *[1 mark]* (approximately three sets of 12-15 reps). Overload by gradually increasing the number of reps *[1 mark]*.

2   (a) E.g. Circuit training can be tailored to improve lots of different components of fitness in one session *[1 mark]*.

(b) E.g. Skipping *[1 mark]*

(c) E.g. He could hold weights to increase the resistance *[1 mark]*.
He could also do more repetitions.

3   E.g. She can ensure students are wearing the correct protective clothing, like shin pads and gum shields *[1 mark]*. She can ensure students are wearing the correct footwear so they don't slip *[1 mark]*. She can ensure that students are using the correct technique for hitting the ball *[1 mark]*.

4   E.g. Static stretching improves flexibility and increases the range of movement at a joint, which can help an endurance athlete to perform more efficiently *[1 mark]*. Stretching can help to prevent delayed onset muscle soreness after a long training run, so the athlete recovers more quickly *[1 mark]*. However, static stretching doesn't mimic the running action used by an endurance athlete *[1 mark]*. Other training methods are more important for endurance athletes, e.g. continuous training is needed to improve cardiovascular endurance and muscular endurance *[1 mark]*.
You can't get all four marks if you only give benefits (or limitations) of static stretching for endurance athletes, so make sure you consider both.

5   *This mark scheme gives examples of some points you might have made in your answer, and how many marks you'd get for making those points. You can still get full marks if you haven't written every individual point below, as long as the points you've made are detailed enough.*

You will get up to two marks for showing knowledge and understanding of interval training and continuous training, for example:
- Interval training involves alternating periods of high- and low-intensity exercise.
- Continuous training involves training at a constant rate without any rests.

You will get up to four marks if you also apply knowledge of these training methods to a basketball player, for example:
- Interval training is suitable for a basketball player as they need to run at different intensities throughout a match.
- Continuous training improves cardiovascular endurance, which is important for a basketball player, as a basketball match involves aerobic activity.

You will get up to nine marks if you also justify why interval training and continuous training are suitable for a basketball player, for example:
- Basketball requires sudden spurts of fast movement to beat an opponent to the ball. Interval training can help prepare the player for this by combining slower jogs with quicker sprints within one training session.
- Continuous training improves cardiovascular endurance, which will help the basketball player to use their muscles continuously throughout a game without tiring too much.
- Interval training is well suited to the conditions of a basketball game, with its constantly changing pace. Therefore interval training is a crucial part of a basketball player's training.
- Continuous training is an important part of a basketball player's training as it helps to prepare them for constantly moving throughout the game.
- Continuous training does not improve anaerobic fitness required by a basketball player.
- Both types of training can be used effectively by a basketball player, however it would be sensible for a basketball player to also use weight training and plyometric training to develop the strength and power they need.
[9 marks available in total]

Section Four — Sports Psychology

Page 61 (Warm-Up Questions)

1) A performer's ability is their set of traits that control their potential to learn a skill.
2) A skill that needs lots of decision-making, so requires a lot of thought and coordination.
3) E.g. A free throw in basketball.
4) A performance goal is a target aimed at improving your own personal performance.
5) E.g. It might be difficult for a performer to achieve an outcome goal, as it will depend on how well other people perform.
6) Measurable
7) A target needs to be accepted because the other people involved (e.g. a coach) can make sure the target is set at the right level of difficulty.

Page 62 (Exam Questions)

1 (a) E.g. If a goal is measurable, then a performer can see how much they have progressed towards achieving it *[1 mark]*. This can help to motivate a performer to continue training hard, so that their performance will continue to improve *[1 mark]*.
   (b) It specifies a time and a distance, both of which can be accurately measured *[1 mark]*.
   (c) E.g. Layla could make her goal time-bound by setting a deadline for when she wants to achieve it, for example, within two months *[1 mark]*. This will help increase her motivation to train, as she will know how much she needs to improve in a certain amount of time *[1 mark]*. Layla could also make sure her goal is accepted by discussing her goal with other people involved, such as a coach *[1 mark]*. This will make sure her goal is set at the right level of difficulty, so that she will stay motivated to continue training *[1 mark]*.

2 E.g. Complex — it requires lots of thought and coordination to perform *[1 mark]*.
   Closed — it involves the same action each time *[1 mark]*.
   Self-paced — you decide when to do the somersault *[1 mark]*.
   Gross — it involves large muscle groups in the arms and legs *[1 mark]*.
   You can say that the skill belongs to a different classification, as long as your explanation is suitable. E.g. Externally-paced — a coach or judge might decide when it should be performed.

Page 67 (Warm-Up Questions)

1) Any **one** from: e.g.
   - It can be combined with other guidance types.
   - It's useful for explaining techniques to elite performers, as they will understand the language used.
   - It can be given during a performance.
2) Extrinsic feedback comes from a source that is not the performer, for example, a coach or teammate.
3) E.g. Beginners need to be told whether or not they achieved the right result.
4) The output stage is when a skill is performed. This is done by the brain sending messages to the muscles to tell them how to move.
5) Someone's arousal level is how mentally and physically alert they are.
6) E.g. A boxer throwing a punch at their opponent.
7) An extrovert is more likely to play rugby than an introvert.

Pages 68-69 (Exam Questions)

1 **A** Putting a ball in golf *[1 mark]*
2 **C** Often thoughtful *[1 mark]*
3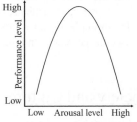

[1 mark for correctly labelled x-axis and y-axis, 1 mark for correct shape of inverted-U graph]

4 E.g. Knowledge of performance feedback would be effective because Katarina is an elite level performer who knows the correct technique for a hammer throw *[1 mark]*. Knowledge of performance feedback will help to improve/fine-tune movements of the hammer throw, e.g. the footwork, which would be needed to perfect it at an elite level *[1 mark]*.

5 (a) Any **two** from:
     • Mental rehearsal
     • Visualisation
     • Deep breathing
     • Imagery
     • Positive self-talk/thinking
     [1 mark for each up to a maximum of 2 marks]

   (b) E.g. A footballer may need to use a stress management technique before taking a penalty *[1 mark]*, as an arousal level that is too high could cause them to become nervous and take a poor penalty *[1 mark]*.

6 *This mark scheme gives examples of some points you might have made in your answer, and how many marks you'd get for making those points. You can still get full marks if you haven't written every individual point below, as long as the points you've made are detailed enough.*

   You will get one mark for showing knowledge and understanding of the different stages of the information processing model, for example:
   • The four stages of the information processing model are input, decision making, output and feedback.

   You will get up to three marks if you also apply knowledge of the information processing model to a football tackle, for example:
   • Input is the player seeing the opponent running with the ball.
   • Decision making is the player deciding how to tackle.
   • Output is the tackle that is performed.
   • Feedback is information about how the tackle was performed.

   You will get up to six marks if you also analyse characteristics of the different stages of the information processing model in relation to a football tackle, for example:
   • During the input stage, the footballer will receive information, such as how fast their opponent is running and which direction they are going in.
   • During the input stage, the footballer might use selective attention to block out distractions (e.g. noise from the crowd), so they can focus on tackling their opponent.
   • During the decision making stage, the footballer will access their long-term memory to refer to previous experiences of performing different types of tackle successfully.
   • During the decision making stage, the footballer will use their short-term memory to analyse what is happening in the game at the time, before deciding how to tackle.
   • During the output stage, information is sent from the footballer's brain to the muscles in their legs, such as the hamstrings and quadriceps, telling them how to carry out the tackle.
   • During the feedback stage, the footballer receives either intrinsic feedback from themselves, or extrinsic feedback from their coach or teammates. For example, whether they gained possession of the ball or used the correct technique.
   [6 marks available in total]

Section Five — Sport, Society and Culture

Page 74 (Warm-Up Questions)

1) E.g. Your parents might encourage you to take up sports, which will give you more opportunities to participate. Also, your siblings might play or be interested in sport, so you are familiar with it from a young age and so are more likely to play it yourself.

2) E.g. Role models can inspire people to take up a sport.

3) E.g. Religious beliefs about the Sabbath may prevent someone playing sport on certain days. This could limit the opportunities they have to participate in a particular sport.

4) E.g. Adapting sports so that they're more accessible for disabled people.

5) A socio-economic group is a way of grouping people based on how much money they have, where they live and the type of job they do.

6) E.g. Having the chance to try out a range of activities might help you to find a sport you enjoy and encourage you to exercise. If you dislike competitive sports, some PE lessons might put you off doing exercise.

Page 75 (Exam Questions)

1 **C** Cost *[1 mark]*

2 Any **two** from: e.g.
   • There may be fewer opportunities through lack of facilities and equipment.
   • They may face discrimination or stereotypes about disabled people which may discourage them from taking part.
   • The lack of media coverage of disabled sporting events compared to other sporting events may mean there are fewer role models to inspire people to take part.
   [1 mark for each up to a maximum of 2 marks]

3 *This mark scheme gives examples of some points you might have made in your answer, and how many marks you'd get for making those points. You can still get full marks if you haven't written every individual point below, as long as the points you've made are detailed enough.*

   You will get one mark for showing knowledge and understanding of the influences on sport participation, for example:
   • Participation in sport can be influenced by factors such as role models, socio-economic groups, family/friends and accessibility.

   You will get up to three marks if you also apply these influences to Jake, for example:
   • There might be a lack of role models to inspire Jake to take part in sport.
   • Jake may be from a lower socio-economic group.
   • Jake may not have any friends who take part in sport.
   • Jake's family may not encourage him to take part in sport.
   • Jake may have developed a negative attitude towards sport.

   You will get up to six marks if you also justify your choices of influences on Jake, for example:
   • Jake may have had a bad experience in school PE lessons that has put him off participating in sport.
   • Jake's family might not have the money to afford the necessary clothing/equipment to take part in sport.
   • There might be a lack of facilities available in Jake's local area, so he could be prevented from participating in a particular sport.
   • Jake's family may not enjoy sport so he may not have been exposed to sport from a young age.
   • Jake may be influenced by the negative attitude of his PE teacher or his friends.
   [6 marks available in total]

Page 80 (Warm-Up Questions)

1) The commercialisation of sport means managing sport in a way designed to make profit.

2) E.g. Newspapers, television and radio.

3) False

4) E.g. A company may provide a performer with branded clothing / equipment to advertise their company name or logo.

5) E.g. They may have to appear in adverts, even if they don't want to.

6) E.g. Their products are harmful. A sports team may not want to promote these companies as they give a false image of health.

7) E.g. Better protective clothing, playing surfaces and medical technology can all help players to avoid injury.

8) E.g. Some technologies, e.g. Hawkeye, disrupt the flow of play, which can be boring for spectators.

Page 81 (Exam Questions)

1 **B** Holidays *[1 mark]*

2 *This mark scheme gives examples of some points you might have made in your answer, and how many marks you'd get for making those points. You can still get full marks if you haven't written every individual point below, as long as the points you've made are detailed enough.*

You will get up to two marks for showing knowledge and understanding of the commercialisation of sport, for example:
- The commercialisation of sport means that there is more money available.
- A lot of this money comes through sponsorship deals, where companies pay to have their logo associated with a team or performer.
- Money also comes from the media, who pay for the rights to cover the sport.

You will get up to four marks if you also give effects of commercialisation on performers and spectators, for example:
- Increased commercialisation of sport has lead to more valuable sponsorship deals for performers.
- Commercialisation of sport has lead to increased media attention on performers.
- Commercialisation of sport means the media can control when and how often sporting events take place.
- Commercialisation of sport means the media can educate spectators on the rules of the sport.

You will get up to nine marks if you also evaluate whether the impact of commercialisation on performers and spectators has been positive or negative, for example:
- Increased media coverage of performers can make them into role models, who can inspire people from different backgrounds to participate in sport.
- Commercialisation has had some positive impact on performers, for example, very high earnings due to the increase in the value of sponsorship deals.
- Sponsorship deals mean that performers may have to appear in adverts and endorse products, even if they don't want to.
- Performers have a lack of privacy due to media coverage of their private lives. The media's control of how often matches are played can also impact performers negatively, as it means they could be more likely to get injured.
- Spectators might miss out on seeing games live if the media decide when they are to be broadcast, but can catch up on games in their own time if they miss out.
- Broadcasting live events on the television/Internet can reduce the number of spectators at the event, making the atmosphere poorer.
- Commercialisation has had a positive impact on performers and spectators. Performers have to sacrifice some of their privacy, but can earn large amounts of money and can therefore play their sport full-time. Spectators have more opportunities to watch sport in their own time.
[9 marks available in total]

Page 85 (Warm-Up Questions)

1) E.g. Gamesmanship means gaining an advantage by using tactics that push the rules without breaking them, whereas sportsmanship means playing within the rules, upholding the spirit of the game and using sports etiquette.

2) E.g. A footballer kicking the ball out of play if an opposition player has an injury.

3) False

4) E.g. A positive affect of anabolic agents is that they increase bone and muscle growth. But a negative effect is that they can cause heart disease.

5) E.g. To kill pain, so injuries and fatigue don't affect performance.

6) E.g. EPO causes the body to produce more red blood cells. Endurance athletes, e.g. road racing cyclists, would benefit.

7) E.g. Crowds can create a good atmosphere which can make the game more enjoyable for the players, and can create a 'home-field advantage' for the home team.

8) E.g. Fans are less packed together which makes it easier for stewards and police to get to the fans causing trouble.

Pages 86-87 (Exam Questions)

1 **B** Shaking hands with opponents and officials after a match *[1 mark]*

2 **C** Increasing stadium capacity *[1 mark]*

3 E.g. Using a PED increases the chance of a performer achieving success in their sport *[1 mark]*. If caught using a PED, a performer may be banned from competing *[1 mark]*.
Other advantages here include fame, wealth and creating a level playing field. Disadvantages include reputational damage and fines.

4 E.g. A shot-putter will have greater performance gains from anabolic agents *[1 mark]* because throwing the shot requires a large amount of strength and power, so performers need a large muscle mass *[1 mark]*.

5 E.g. The coach calling a timeout just before the opponent takes the free throw is an example of gamesmanship *[1 mark]*. This is because the coach is gaining an advantage by trying to make the opponent overthink the free throw, but calling a timeout at that point doesn't break the rules *[1 mark]*.
A deliberate foul breaks the rules, so this is not gamesmanship.

6 (a) Any **two** from: e.g.
- Blood thickening
- Potential infection
- Increased risk of heart attack
- Blocked blood vessels (embolism)
[1 mark for each up to a maximum of 2 marks]

(b) E.g. Blood doping could benefit a long-distance runner *[1 mark]* because it increases the number of red blood cells in the bloodstream *[1 mark]*, which increases oxygen supply to the muscles, and improves cardiovascular endurance *[1 mark]*.

7 E.g. Spectators create an atmosphere which adds to the excitement *[1 mark]*. This can create a 'home-field advantage' where the 'home' team performs better because they are in familiar surroundings with more fans supporting them *[1 mark]*. However, more spectators creates more pressure for sportspeople to perform *[1 mark]* and there is the potential for hooliganism from spectators *[1 mark]*.
You can't get all four marks if you only give positive (or negative) effects of spectators at sporting events, so make sure you consider both.

Section Six — Health, Fitness and Well-being

Page 92 (Warm-Up Questions)

1) It can lower blood pressure.

2) E.g. It makes muscles and bones stronger and joints more flexible.

3) E.g. Serotonin is a feel good hormone released during exercise. It can make an individual feel happier, so can improve their mental health and well-being.

4) E.g. Exercise can create a feeling of having achieved something, for example, if a goal is achieved. This would lead to an increase in self-esteem as a performer would have a higher opinion of themselves and feel more confident.

5) Any **one** from: e.g.
   • Obesity
   • Heart disease
   • Diabetes
   • Hypertension (high blood pressure)

6) E.g. Being overweight limits agility. An overweight tennis player would find it difficult to change direction quickly to get to the ball.

7) Obese

Page 93 (Exam Questions)

1 **D** Regular exercise can help you to reduce stress and tension *[1 mark]*

2 (a) E.g. A sedentary lifestyle is one where there is irregular or no physical activity *[1 mark]*.

   (b) Any **three** from: e.g.
   • Obesity
   • Heart disease
   • High blood pressure (hypertension)
   • Diabetes
   • Lethargy
   • Poor sleep
   • Emotional health problems
   • Poor social health
   [1 mark for each up to a maximum of 3 marks]

3 E.g. Exercise improves fitness, which would aid an individual's ability to do manual labour *[1 mark]*. Exercise benefits the musculo-skeletal system — stronger muscles and more flexible joints would make injury less likely *[1 mark]*.

Page 97 (Warm-Up Questions)

1) 55-60%

2) Calories (Kcal)

3) Any **three** from: e.g.
   • Age
   • Gender
   • Height
   • Exercise levels

4) E.g. Minerals help to keep bones and teeth strong.

5) Any **two** from: e.g.
   • Blood thickening
   • Increased heart rate
   • Slower reactions
   • Increase in body temperature
   • Muscle fatigue / cramps

6) Ectomorph

7) E.g. Wrestling

Page 98 (Exam Questions)

1 **B** 55-60% carbohydrates, 25-30% fats, 15-20% proteins *[1 mark]*

2 (a) Mesomorph *[1 mark]*

   (b) E.g. Abby would be suited to weightlifting *[1 mark]*. As a mesomorph, Abby has broad shoulders which makes it easier for her to support weight using her upper body *[1 mark]*.
   There are other examples you could have mentioned, such as sprinting, tennis or gymnastics.

3 *This mark scheme gives examples of some points you might have made in your answer, and how many marks you'd get for making those points. You can still get full marks if you haven't written every individual point below, as long as the points you've made are detailed enough.*

   You will get one mark for showing knowledge and understanding of the role of carbohydrates and fats, for example:
   • Carbohydrates can be used as an energy source for any intensity of exercise.
   • Fats can be used as an energy source for low-intensity exercise.

   You will get up to three marks if you also apply knowledge of carbohydrates and fats to a marathon runner, for example:
   • Carbohydrates would be used for the majority of a marathon, as they are the main energy source for the body.
   • Fats could be used when running very slowly during a marathon.

   You will get up to six marks if you also evaluate the importance of carbohydrates and fats for a marathon runner, for example:
   • Carbohydrates are essential for a marathon runner to provide energy for moderate-intensity parts of the race and high-intensity parts of the race, such as steep climbs, or when overtaking other runners.
   • A marathon runner would benefit from some fats in their diet as they provide more energy than carbohydrates at low intensity, e.g. during slower parts of the race.
   • A diet too high in fats could cause a marathon runner to gain weight. This would reduce their cardiovascular endurance and their speed, so would have a negative effect on performance.
   • A diet with some fat and plenty of carbohydrates would be most suitable for a marathon runner.
   [6 marks available in total]

Section Seven — Using Data

Page 104 (Warm-Up Questions)

1) E.g. Fitness testing and surveys.

2) E.g. If a line graph slopes upwards from left to right, then the values on the y-axis are generally increasing as you move along the x-axis.

3) E.g. Fitness testing data can tell you whether your training is working or not. If the data shows you are doing better at a fitness test over time, it suggests your fitness is increasing.

Page 105 (Exam Questions)

1 (a) E.g. It shows quantitative data *[1 mark]* because the graph shows the number of people who participated in different activities *[1 mark]*.

   (b) E.g. Participation in running is likely to decrease in 22/23 *[1 mark]* because it has decreased each year since 16/17 except 19/20, so you would expect the trend to continue *[1 mark]*.

(c) Cycling *[1 mark]*.

E.g. Reduced media coverage of elite cyclists *[1 mark]* may have decreased the number of role models to inspire people to take up cycling *[1 mark]*.

You may have mentioned a different reason here — as long as you can justify your reason, you'll get the marks.

Practice Papers

Pages 107–119 (Practice Paper 1)

1 **C** Tibia *[1 mark]*

2 **B** Triceps *[1 mark]*

3 **D** The effort is between the fulcrum and load *[1 mark]*

4 **A** Flexion *[1 mark]*

5 **B** Cardiovascular endurance *[1 mark]*

6 **D** Circuit training *[1 mark]*

7 **C** Alveoli have access to a large blood supply *[1 mark]*

8 E.g. Tendons attach muscle to bone *[1 mark]*. When muscles contract, the tendons pull the bones to move the skeleton *[1 mark]*.

9.1 E.g. Blood is redistributed around the body when the arterioles supplying the muscles widen (and arterioles supplying inactive areas of the body constrict) *[1 mark]*. This causes the amount of blood flowing to the muscles used during exercise to increase *[1 mark]*.

9.2 Any **two** from:
- Increased blood pressure
- Increased heart rate
- Increased stroke volume
- Increased cardiac output

[1 mark for each up to a maximum of 2 marks]

10.1 E.g.

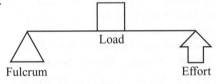

[1 mark for fulcrum, load and effort labelled in the correct order]

10.2 The lever has a high mechanical advantage, so can move the weight of the body with small effort *[1 mark]*. However, it only allows a small range of movement *[1 mark]*.

11 E.g. marathon running:
- A stronger heart (cardiac hypertrophy) would increase cardiac output. More blood and oxygen to the muscles means that performers could run for longer.
- Muscle hypertrophy would improve muscular endurance. Performers would be able to run for longer before their muscles start to fatigue.

[2 marks available in total — 1 mark for each benefit]

You'll likely have used a different example here — you'll need to have related the long-term benefits of exercise to your example to get the marks.

12.1 Any **two** from: e.g.
- Ligaments hold bones together / restrict how much a joint moves.
- Cartilage helps bones move smoothly.
- Synovial membrane releases synovial fluid.
- Synovial fluid lubricates the joint.
- Bursae reduce friction between bones / tissues.
- The ends of bones are shaped so they fit together with other bones.

[1 mark for each up to a maximum of 2 marks]

12.2 Flexion *[1 mark]*

12.3 E.g. The antagonistic muscle pair at the knee works to push the athlete's body weight off the floor *[1 mark]* as the quadriceps contract *[1 mark]* and the hamstrings relax *[1 mark]*.

13 E.g. Anaerobic respiration can release energy very quickly for short periods, allowing a performer to sprint through the water *[1 mark]*. This makes it very useful during races of a short distance, or in parts of longer races, such as a sprint finish *[1 mark]*. However, anaerobic respiration releases lactic acid as a by-product *[1 mark]*, which would eventually lead to muscle fatigue, so it can't be sustained for a long period *[1 mark]*.

Don't just talk about the positives — you'll need at least one negative effect of anaerobic respiration too for full marks.

14.1 $220 - 40 = 180$ bpm *[1 mark]*

14.2 Upper anaerobic threshold:
180×0.9 *[1 mark]* $= 162$ bpm *[1 mark]*
Lower anaerobic threshold:
180×0.8 *[1 mark]* $= 144$ bpm *[1 mark]*

15.1 E.g. Sit on the floor with your legs straight in front of you and feet flat against a box. Reach as far as you can, and measure how many centimetres past your toes you have reached using a tape measure.
[2 marks for a complete description, 1 mark for a partial description]

15.2 E.g. Flexibility is the amount of movement possible at a joint *[1 mark]*. Having a high level of flexibility in, for example, the hip joint, would help a long jumper to reach their legs further *[1 mark]*, and therefore jump a greater distance *[1 mark]*.

15.3 E.g. Put chalk on your fingertips and, standing side-on to a wall, mark the highest point you can reach. Jump as high as you can and mark the highest point reached on the wall. Measure the distance between the two marks.
[2 marks for a complete description, 1 mark for a partial description]

15.4 E.g. The vertical jump test measures leg power which is an important component of fitness for a beach volleyball player *[1 mark]*. It specifically measures the ability to jump high, which is important for skills such as spiking the ball *[1 mark]*. However, other components of fitness are also important for beach volleyball, such as reaction time or agility *[1 mark]*.
You might agree that the vertical jump test is important, but to get full marks you also need to consider limitations of the test or suggest other components of fitness or tests that would be needed.

16 E.g. rugby union:
- Helps maintain components of fitness needed for matches (e.g. cardiovascular endurance, strength) and avoid reversibility.
- Can develop specific skills to help performance, e.g. improving kicks could help a performer score more drop goals.

[1 mark for each up to a maximum of 2 marks]

17 E.g.
- Rugby players should tackle with the correct technique and timing *[1 mark]* to avoid being hit by a trailing foot *[1 mark]*.
- Rugby players should wear the recommended protective equipment, such as shin pads or a scrum cap *[1 mark]*. Protective equipment is designed to protect the most vulnerable body areas for that sport *[1 mark]*.

18.1 Progressive overload means gradually increasing the amount of overload done in training to increase fitness without risk of injury *[1 mark]*.

18.2 E.g. If a javelin thrower used weight training, they could gradually increase the weight lifted *[1 mark]* in order to increase their strength *[1 mark]*.

18.3 E.g. Milly's training applies specificity in some ways, as it focuses specifically on training the muscle groups in the legs, which are used constantly throughout a hockey match *[1 mark]*. It will also improve her cardiovascular endurance, which will enable her to move continuously throughout the match without becoming tired *[1 mark]*. However, it does not completely apply specificity, as jogging will not improve the skills that are specific to hockey, such as shooting accurately at the goal *[1 mark]*. *You can't get all three marks if you only agree (or disagree) that her training applies specificity, so make sure you consider both arguments.*

19 E.g.
- 0 to 20 minutes: he may have been jogging lightly to warm up *[1 mark]* because his heart rate increases for 10 minutes, then stays at a moderate rate *[1 mark]* between 10 and 20 minutes.
- 20 to 50 minutes: he may have increased his running speed and then continued to run at this speed *[1 mark]*, because his heart rate increases very quickly and stays elevated to this level between 20 and 50 minutes *[1 mark]*.

20.1 E.g. Use a low weight, below 70% of one rep max, with a high number of reps (about three sets of 12-15 reps) *[1 mark]*. Overload is produced by gradually increasing the number of repetitions *[1 mark]*.

20.2 E.g.

Advantage	Disadvantage
Can be adapted to focus on specific muscle groups for different activities *[1 mark]*.	Can be dangerous if a participant has a poor technique *[1 mark]*.

21 *This mark scheme gives examples of some points you might have made in your answer, and how many marks you would get for making those points. You can still get full marks if you haven't written every individual point below, as long as the points you have made are detailed enough.*

You will get one mark for showing knowledge and understanding of muscular endurance and agility, for example:
- Muscular endurance is the ability to use the body's muscles for a long time without becoming tired.
- Agility is the ability to change body position or direction quickly and with control.

You will get up to three marks if you also apply knowledge of muscular endurance and agility to netball, for example:
- A netball player would need good muscular endurance to be able to use their leg and arm muscles for the duration of a netball match.
- A netball player would need agility to move quickly around the court to find space / to receive a pass / to mark an opponent.

You will get up to six marks if you also evaluate the importance of muscular endurance and agility for performers in netball, for example:
- Good muscular endurance is important in netball, as it would prevent a player's muscles from fatiguing towards the end of a match. This would allow them to continue to run quickly around the court and pass and shoot the ball powerfully.
- Agility is very important for many aspects of a netball match, such as intercepting and making passes. Both of these skills give your team more possession of the ball and greater chances to score.
- Both muscular endurance and agility would benefit performers in netball. However, a netball player may also want to focus on improving other components of fitness. For example, improved hand-eye coordination would mean they could shoot more accurately, and therefore score more goals.

[6 marks available in total]

22 *This mark scheme gives examples of some points you might have made in your answer, and how many marks you would get for making those points. You can still get full marks if you haven't written every individual point below, as long as the points you have made are detailed enough.*

You will get up to two marks for showing knowledge and understanding of tidal volume, for example:
- Tidal volume is the volume of air breathed in or out during one breath.
- Tidal volume increases during exercise.

You will get up to four marks if you also apply your knowledge of tidal volume to a midfielder during a football match, for example:
- Tidal volume would be at about the normal rate at the beginning of a match.
- Tidal volume would increase during a match as a midfielder jogs around the pitch, e.g. to get into position to receive passes.
- Tidal volume would greatly increase as the midfielder sprints, e.g. during a counterattack.

You will get up to nine marks if you also evaluate the importance of changes in tidal volume for the performance of a midfielder. You could also include other factors needed to perform well. For example:
- An increase in tidal volume would be necessary to bring in extra oxygen to deliver to the muscles.
- An increase in tidal volume would be necessary to remove carbon dioxide from the muscles more quickly.
- An increase in tidal volume would help the midfielder to remain active for the duration of a match.
- A large increase in tidal volume would help a midfielder to remove lactic acid from the muscles and recover from oxygen debt after sprinting. The muscles wouldn't get fatigued so they could continue to play.
- Other changes would also be necessary to meet the increased oxygen demand in the muscles, for example, increased heart rate, stroke volume and cardiac output, which result in more blood and oxygen being delivered to working muscles.

[9 marks available in total]

Pages 120–131 (Practice Paper 2)

1 **D** 55-60% *[1 mark]*

2 **C** Accepted *[1 mark]*

3 **A** Feedback from how a performance feels to the performer *[1 mark]*

4 **D** When a learner listens to an explanation of how to perform a technique *[1 mark]*

5 **A** Time-wasting in football *[1 mark]*

6 **A** Rugby player *[1 mark]*

7.1 Any **two** from: e.g.
- Improves heart function
- Improves efficiency of the body systems
- Helps to maintain a healthy weight and avoid obesity
- Reduces the risk of illness / disease
- Makes everyday tasks easier to do

[1 mark for each up to a maximum of 2 marks]

7.2 E.g. Exercise increases the level of serotonin in the brain *[1 mark]*, which can make you feel happier *[1 mark]*.
You could have also mentioned that exercise helps to reduce stress or lets you control your emotions.

7.3 Social *[1 mark]*

8.1 Any **two** from:
- Blood becomes thicker (more viscous)
- Increases heart rate
- Slower reactions
- Body temperature increases
- Muscle fatigue / cramps

[1 mark for each up to a maximum of 2 marks]

8.2 E.g. long distance running:
Dehydration could cause muscle fatigue, which makes muscles tired and painful *[1 mark]*. This would mean a runner would be unable to perform as well, as they would be forced to either run more slowly or stop completely *[1 mark]*.

9.1 E.g. For some people from certain ethnic groups there may be a lack of role models in sport *[1 mark]*. This could lead some people to be less inspired to participate in sport themselves *[1 mark]*.

9.2 Any **two** from: e.g.
- Age
- Socio-economic group
- Disability
- Experiences in PE at school
- Attitudes of family / friends

[1 mark for each up to a maximum of 2 marks]

10.1 E.g. A lifestyle with irregular or no physical activity *[1 mark]*.

10.2 If more energy is taken in than is used, the spare energy will be stored as fat *[1 mark]*. An increase in fat will cause weight gain, which can lead to obesity *[1 mark]*.

10.3 E.g. Obesity limits cardiovascular endurance *[1 mark]*. He would not be able to get oxygen to the muscles quickly, so would not be able to swim for a long period of time *[1 mark]*.

Obesity limits flexibility *[1 mark]*. A lack of flexibility at the shoulders would restrict his arm movements, so his swimming strokes would be less efficient *[1 mark]*.

11 E.g. A trophy is an example of extrinsic motivation *[1 mark]*. Performers may push themselves to win a trophy because it will make them feel proud / good about themselves *[1 mark]*.

12.1 E.g.

Advantage	Disadvantage
Manual guidance will help the gymnast get a feel of the skill before trying to perform it on their own *[1 mark]*.	The gymnast may begin to rely on the manual guidance and be unable to perform a cartwheel on the beam without the coach's help *[1 mark]*.

12.2 E.g. The gymnast could use deep breathing to reduce their heart rate / nerves at the start of the routine *[1 mark]*.

They could also use mental rehearsal to picture carrying out the complex skills of the routine perfectly *[1 mark]*.

12.3 E.g. A mesomorph *[1 mark]* is most suited for gymnastics because gymnasts need broad shoulders to support their own body weight *[1 mark]*.

13 E.g. Amanda's goal applies the time-bound principle by saying that she wants to achieve her goal in four months *[1 mark]*. Having a deadline will help motivate her to train *[1 mark]* and will therefore improve her fitness and performance so she will be more likely to achieve her goal *[1 mark]*.

14.1 Any **one** from: e.g.
- Creates an atmosphere
- Creates a home-field advantage

[1 mark for a suitable answer]

14.2 Any **two** from: e.g.
- Rivalry between fans of the teams
- Spectators drinking alcohol before the match
- Frustration at refereeing decisions
- Display of masculinity

[1 mark for each up to a maximum of 2 marks]

15.1 E.g. A skill is a learned action to bring about the result you want with certainty and minimum effort *[1 mark]*.

15.2 E.g. Catching is a fine skill as it involves the use of small muscle groups in the arm / wrist and requires precision *[1 mark]*. Catching a cricket ball is externally-paced as it will depend on the delivery of the ball and if / how the batsman strikes it *[1 mark]*.
You could also argue that catching can be a gross skill if a wicket-keeper has to dive to reach to the ball.

15.3 E.g.
Input: sight of the cricket ball moving towards the wicket-keeper *[1 mark]*.
Decision making: choice of how to position the hands to catch the ball from memory *[1 mark]*.
Output: muscles move in the arms / hands to a catching position *[1 mark]*.
Feedback: intrinsic feedback based on whether the ball was caught *[1 mark]*.

16 E.g. Figure 2a shows that more women participate in swimming than men *[1 mark]*. This could be because there are more female role models in swimming than male role models *[1 mark]*. Figure 2b shows that more men participate in football than women *[1 mark]*. This could be because some women have faced discrimination for wanting to play football *[1 mark]*.

17.1 E.g. Gamesmanship is gaining an advantage by using tactics that push the rules without breaking them *[1 mark]*.

17.2 E.g. Elite performers demonstrating gamesmanship could be bad for sport as it could lead to more occurrences of gamesmanship at lower levels of the sport *[1 mark]*. This is because elite performers are role models and cricket is a high-profile sport *[1 mark]*, so their behaviour would gain lots of media attention and may inspire others to behave in the same way *[1 mark]*.

17.3 E.g. Blood doping involves removing blood from a performer a few weeks before competition *[1 mark]*. It is frozen and then re-injected into the performer just before competition *[1 mark]*.

17.4 E.g. Anabolic agents would give the most significant performance benefit to a 100 m sprinter *[1 mark]* as they increase muscle growth and therefore strength *[1 mark]*, which sprinters need in order to generate the necessary power to sprint quickly *[1 mark]*.

18 E.g. Financial sponsorship of a team would mean that they would have more money *[1 mark]*. They would spend this money on improved equipment or facilities *[1 mark]*, which may help them to improve their performance *[1 mark]*.

19 *This mark scheme gives examples of some points you might have made in your answer, and how many marks you would get for making those points. You can still get full marks if you haven't written every individual point below, as long as the points you have made are detailed enough.*

You will get one mark for showing knowledge and understanding of the different types of media, for example:
- The different types of media include television, radio, newspapers (the press), the Internet and social media.

You will get up to three marks if you also apply knowledge of different types of media to examples in sport, for example:
- The media pay to broadcast sporting events on TV, e.g. Premier League football matches.
- Social media allows people to follow their favourite sports stars.
- Many people have access to the Internet, which means sports reach a global audience.

You will get up to six marks if you also evaluate the impact of increased media interest on sport, for example:
- TV / internet coverage can increase awareness of a sport, which could lead to an increase in participation of that sport.
- Newspaper articles on elite performers can create role models and inspire people to participate in sport.
- Television companies / sports broadcasters provide investment into sport, which can be used to develop facilities at lower levels.
- Television companies / sports broadcasters are in a position of power if a sport becomes reliant on their money. They could dictate when and how games are played or change the rules of the sport.
- Discussion and analysis of refereeing decisions on social media can put officials under pressure.

[6 marks available in total]

20 *This mark scheme gives examples of some points you might have made in your answer, and how many marks you would get for making those points. You can still get full marks if you haven't written every individual point below, as long as the points you have made are detailed enough.*

You will get up to two marks for showing knowledge and understanding of visual and mechanical guidance, for example:
- Visual guidance involves being shown visually how to perform a skill.
- Mechanical guidance involves the use of equipment to help a learner perform a skill.

You will get up to four marks if you also apply your knowledge of visual and mechanical guidance to a group of beginners in trampolining, for example:
- Visual guidance could be used to demonstrate how basic bounces on the trampoline should look.
- Mechanical guidance could include the use of a harness to guide the learners through a somersault on the trampoline.

You will get up to nine marks if you also make justifications for the use of visual and mechanical guidance to coach a group of beginners in trampolining, for example:
- Visual guidance would be useful for the beginners who aren't familiar with different trampolining skills.
- Visual guidance would be useful for beginners as they would be able to copy basic skills, such as bouncing, from demonstrations.
- Mechanical guidance can be very useful for a beginner in trampolining, as it can increase their confidence at performing more dangerous skills.
- Mechanical guidance works well to teach complex skills, and is therefore well suited for teaching trampolining, as many of the skills in the sport can be classified as complex skills.
- Mechanical guidance, such as a harness, could take a long time to set up, so would be time-consuming if teaching a large group.
- It may be best for visual guidance to be used initially so that the beginners can become familiar with what trampolining skills should look like, before using mechanical guidance to help them learn the skill.
- Other types of guidance, such as verbal guidance could also be used with visual and mechanical guidance to provide more help for the beginners.

[9 marks available in total]

Glossary

abduction	Movement away from an imaginary centre line through the body.
ability	A person's set of traits that control their potential to learn a skill.
adduction	Movement towards an imaginary centre line through the body.
aerobic exercise	Exercise in the presence of or using oxygen.
agility	The ability to change body position or direction quickly and with control.
alveoli	Small air bags in the lungs where gases are exchanged.
anaerobic exercise	Exercise in the absence of enough oxygen, or without oxygen.
antagonistic muscle pair	A pair of muscles that work together to bring about movement. As one muscle contracts (the agonist or prime mover) the other relaxes (the antagonist).
arousal	A person's level of mental and physical alertness.
axis of movement	An imaginary line that the body or a body part can move around.
balance	The ability to keep the body's centre of mass over a base of support.
balanced diet	A diet that contains the best ratio of nutrients to match your lifestyle.
basic (simple) skill	A skill which is quick to learn as it doesn't need much thought or decision-making, e.g. running.
blood cell	Component of blood. There are red blood cells (which carry oxygen and carbon dioxide) and white blood cells (which fight disease).
blood pressure	How strongly the blood presses against the walls of blood vessels.
blood vessel	Part of the cardiovascular system that transports blood around the body. The three main types are arteries, veins and capillaries.
Body Mass Index (BMI)	A score used to determine whether a person is underweight, a healthy weight, overweight or obese.
calorie	A unit used to measure the amount of energy in food. It's often shortened to Kcal.
cardiac output	The volume of blood pumped by each ventricle in the heart per minute.
cardio-respiratory system	The combination of the cardiovascular and respiratory systems working together to get oxygen into the body tissues and carbon dioxide out of them.
cardiovascular endurance	The ability of the heart and lungs to supply oxygen to the working muscles.

Glossary

cardiovascular system	The <u>organs</u> responsible for <u>circulating blood</u> around the body.
closed skill	A skill performed in a <u>predictable environment</u> — it's not affected by external factors.
commercialisation	<u>Managing sport</u> in a way designed to make <u>profit</u>, e.g. through <u>sponsorship</u> and the <u>media</u>.
complex skill	A skill which needs <u>lots of decision-making</u> so requires a lot of <u>thought</u> and <u>coordination</u>, e.g. an overhead kick in football.
concentric contraction	A type of isotonic muscle contraction where a muscle contracts and <u>shortens</u>.
connective tissue	Body tissue that <u>holds</u> other body tissues (e.g. muscles and bones) <u>together</u>.
contract to compete	An unwritten <u>agreement</u> between competitors to <u>comply</u> with all the rules (both <u>written</u> and <u>unwritten</u>) and to do their best.
cool-down	<u>Light exercise</u> and <u>stretching</u> done <u>after exercise</u> to return your body to resting levels.
coordination	The ability to use <u>two or more</u> parts of the body <u>together</u>, efficiently and accurately.
data	<u>Information</u> — in <u>words</u> or <u>numbers</u> that can be shown in <u>graphs</u> and <u>tables</u>. Data can be <u>quantitative</u> (numbers) or <u>qualitative</u> (words).
delayed onset of muscle soreness (DOMS)	<u>Soreness</u> in the muscles in the <u>days after exercise</u>.
diffusion	The process of <u>substances</u> (e.g. oxygen) <u>moving</u> from a place where there is a <u>higher concentration</u> to a place where there is a <u>lower concentration</u>.
dorsiflexion	<u>Flexion</u> at the <u>ankle</u> by lifting the toes.
eccentric contraction	A type of isotonic muscle contraction where a muscle contracts and <u>lengthens</u>.
expiratory reserve volume (ERV)	The amount of <u>extra air</u> that can be <u>breathed out</u> after breathing out normally.
extension	<u>Opening a joint</u>, e.g. straightening the leg at the knee.
externally-paced skill	A skill that starts because of <u>external factors</u> which also <u>control the pace</u> of the skill.
feedback	<u>Information</u> about <u>how you did</u> — can be <u>intrinsic</u> (from yourself) or <u>extrinsic</u> (from other sources).
fine skill	A skill using <u>small muscle groups</u> for <u>precise</u> movements requiring <u>accuracy</u> and <u>coordination</u>.
fitness	The ability to meet/cope with the <u>demands</u> of the <u>environment</u>.
flexibility	The amount of <u>movement</u> possible at a <u>joint</u>.
flexion	<u>Closing a joint</u>, e.g. bending the arm at the elbow.

Glossary

gamesmanship	Gaining an <u>advantage</u> by using tactics that <u>push</u> the rules, but <u>don't break them</u>.
gross skill	A skill involving <u>powerful movements</u> performed by <u>large muscle groups</u>.
guidance	<u>Information</u> or <u>help</u> in learning a skill. Guidance can be <u>visual</u>, <u>verbal</u>, <u>manual</u> or <u>mechanical</u>.
health	A state of complete <u>physical</u>, <u>mental</u> and <u>social well-being</u> and not merely the absence of disease or infirmity.
heart rate	The number of times your <u>heart beats</u> in one minute. It is measured in <u>beats per minute</u> (bpm).
hooliganism	<u>Rowdy</u>, <u>aggressive</u> and <u>sometimes violent</u> behaviour of fans and spectators of sport.
hydration	Having the <u>right</u> amount of <u>water</u> for the body to function properly. If you have <u>too little</u> water, you're <u>dehydrated</u>.
inspiratory reserve volume (IRV)	The amount of <u>extra air</u> that can still be <u>breathed in</u> after breathing in normally.
isometric contraction	When a muscle stays the <u>same length</u> as it contracts.
isotonic contraction	When a muscle <u>changes length</u> as it contracts.
joint type	<u>Ball and socket</u> and <u>hinge</u> joints both allow a different <u>range of movement</u>.
lactic acid	A <u>waste product</u> produced during <u>anaerobic respiration</u>, making the muscles feel tired (fatigued).
lever system	A system that allows the body's muscles to move the bones in the skeleton. A lever system can be <u>first</u>, <u>second</u> or <u>third class</u>, and is made up of a <u>lever arm</u>, <u>effort</u>, <u>fulcrum</u> and <u>load</u>.
mechanical advantage	A measure of how <u>efficient</u> a lever is at moving <u>heavy loads</u>.
the media	Organisations involved in <u>mass communication</u> — e.g. through television, radio, newspapers and the Internet.
muscular endurance	The ability to <u>repeatedly</u> use the <u>muscles</u> over a long time, without getting <u>tired</u>.
musculo-skeletal system	The combination of the <u>muscular</u> and <u>skeletal systems</u> working together to allow movement.
obesity	Being <u>obese</u> means having a <u>BMI</u> score of <u>30 or over</u> (for people of white heritage) or <u>27.5 or over</u> (for people in black, Asian or certain other minority ethnic groups).
open skill	A skill performed in a <u>changing environment</u>, where a performer has to <u>react</u> and adapt to <u>external factors</u>.
plane of movement	Imaginary <u>surface</u> used to describe the <u>direction</u> of movement. E.g. sagittal, transverse and frontal.

Glossary

plantar flexion	Extension at the ankle by pointing the toes.
power	A combination of speed and strength.
reaction time	The time taken to move in response to a stimulus.
residual volume	The amount of air left in the lungs after the most possible air has been breathed out.
respiratory system	The organs in the body used for breathing.
rotation	Movement of the body or a body part in a clockwise or anticlockwise motion.
sedentary lifestyle	A lifestyle with irregular or no physical activity.
self-paced skill	A skill controlled by the performer — they decide when and how quickly it's done.
SMART	The five principles of goal setting — specific, measurable, accepted, realistic and time-bound.
socio-economic group	A way of grouping people based on their job, how much money they have and where they live, e.g. 'working class' is a socio-economic group.
somatotype	A person's body type based on their body shape and the amount of muscle and fat they have.
speed	The rate at which someone is able to move, or to cover a distance in a given amount of time.
spirometer trace	A graph produced by a spirometer machine which can be used to measure lung volumes.
sponsorship	The provision of money, equipment, clothing/footwear, or facilities to an individual, team or event in return for some financial gain.
SPORT	The four principles of training — specificity, progressive overload, reversibility and tedium.
sportsmanship	Playing within the rules, upholding the spirit of the game and using sports etiquette.
strength	The amount of force that a muscle or muscle group can apply against a resistance.
stroke volume	The volume of blood pumped with each heartbeat by each ventricle in the heart.
synovial joint	Where two or more bones are joined together in a joint capsule containing synovial fluid.
tidal volume	The amount of air that is breathed in or out in one breath.
training season	Training programmes with different aims depending on whether it's before, during or after the period when sport competition takes place.
training target zone	The range where training is at the right intensity — can be either aerobic (60-80% of maximum heart rate) or anaerobic (80-90% of maximum heart rate).
warm-up	Preparing your body for exercise with pulse-raising activity, stretching and practice actions.

Index

Index